Wake Up, Men!

Other Books by Florence and Fred Littauer

WORD PUBLISHING
Silver Boxes
Dare to Dream (also available in Spanish)
Raising Christians—Not Just Children
Your Personality Tree (also in video album)
Hope for Hurting Women
Looking for God in All the Right Places
Wake Up, Women!

THOMAS NELSON PUBLISHERS
Freeing Your Mind from Memories That Bind (also available in Spanish)
The Promise of Healing
I've Found the Keys, Now Where's the Car?
Get a Life Without the Strife

FLEMING REVELL, BAKER BOOKS
Personality Plus (also available in French, German, and Spanish)
Personality Puzzle (with Marita Littauer)

HARVEST HOUSE PUBLISHERS
Blow Away the Black Clouds
After Every Wedding Comes a Marriage
It Takes So Little to Be Above Average
How to Get Along with Difficult People
Out of the Cabbage Patch

HUNTINGTON HOUSE
Personalities in Power

CLASS BOOKS
Christian Leaders, Authors, and Speakers Seminar (tape, album, and
    manual)
The Best of Florence Littauer

*For information on the Promise of Healing Workshops, CLASS seminars,
or other conferences conducted by Fred and Florence Littauer, please call
1-619-471-0233.*

Wake Up, Men!

HEADSHIP DOESN'T
MEAN LORDSHIP

FRED
LITTAUER

WORD PUBLISHING
Dallas•London•Vancouver•Melbourne

WAKE UP, MEN!

Unless otherwise indicated Scripture quotations are from the King James Version of the Bible. Other Scripture quotations are from:

> The *Good News Bible*, the Bible in Today's English Version (TEV) copyright © 1966, 1971, 1976 American Bible Society. Used by permission.

> The Holy Bible, New International Version (NIV), copyright © 1973, 1978, 1984 International Bible Society. Used by permission of Zondervan Bible Publishers.

> The New American Standard Bible (NASB) © 1960, 1962, 1963, 1968, 1971, 1972, 1973, 1977 by The Lockman Foundation. Used by permission.

> The Living Bible (TLB), copyright 1971 by Tyndale House Publishers, Wheaton, Ill. Used by permission.

Italicized passages of Scripture indicate the author's emphasis.

Stories in this book are based on fact; however, names and details have been changed to protect identities.

Library of Congress Cataloging-in-Publication Data

Littauer, Fred.
     Wake up, men : headship doesn't mean lordship / Fred Littauer.
        p.   cm.
     ISBN 0-8499-3831-7
     1. Husbands. 2. Marriage. 3. Man-woman relationships. I. Title.
HQ756.L55 1994
306.872—dc20   93–42446
                                      CIP

Printed in the United States of America

456789 LB 987654321

CONTENTS

INTRODUCTION

You probably don't think you need this book. *What does he mean, wake up, men? I'm awake. I know what's going on. I don't need some holier-than-thou writer to tell me how to live my life.* Is that what you're thinking? It's what I would have thought a few years ago if someone had given me a book like this.

Someone *did* give it to you, right? Probably it was someone you love—your wife, most likely, or maybe an adult daughter, your mother, or your sister. Or maybe another man recommended it to you after his wife gave it to him.

In all likelihood, it was someone who thought you needed to wake up, take a good look at your life, and make some changes. But he or she was probably afraid to come right out and tell you for fear you would react with anger and denial.

That's how I would have reacted, too, before I woke up.

This book is intended to help Christian men see themselves as they really are and become aware of the damage they may be unintentionally causing their wives and children. In these pages I'll share with you how things used to be in my family, where my wife and children tiptoed around my emotions, withdrawing and trying not to say or do anything that would trigger my angry outbursts. I knew we weren't living the happy, abundant life God intended our family to have, but I couldn't see my part in causing any of the problems. I didn't know how personality differences can affect a marital relationship. I couldn't see the invisible emotional baggage I had carried into our marriage that bound me to unhealthy feelings and prevented me from having the spiritually rich marital and family life God had planned for me.

Finally, with help, I woke up.

Now I've begun to discover the amazing peace, growing fulfillment, and freeing principles of a Spirit-filled marriage. Now, most importantly, I've tapped into the life-changing power of genuine, one-on-one prayer.

For several years my wife, Florence, and I have worked together, traveling around the world to share what we've learned. From the responses we've heard we know these God-inspired ideas have worked for thousands of others, just as they worked for us. They can work for you too.

When you wake up!

1

IS THIS WHAT MARRIAGE IS SUPPOSED TO BE?

I was standing in the foyer of the Riverside Congregational Church in Haverhill, Massachusetts.

Waiting.

It was Saturday evening; our wedding was scheduled to start at seven, and it was already well past that time. *What was the delay?* I sent my brother Steve, my best man, to find out. I wasn't anxious, nervous, or worried. I simply liked things to proceed on schedule. If I had been in charge, they would have been. But I was not in charge.

Finally I got word that my Aunt Edie had not yet arrived from New York. *That* was the delay. I began to feel angry. After all, this was *my* wedding. I wanted to start without her.

But we didn't.

At last, after another half-hour wait, Aunt Edie arrived. The wedding could begin.

The church was packed. Florence was a very popular young English and drama teacher in the local high school. She had put more than a hundred of her students on her wedding committee, and the students kept dreaming up exciting things to make the event unique. One of them had even written to *Life* magazine, asking if the magazine wouldn't like to cover a teacher's wedding where the students were doing all the work. Much to our amazement, *Life* said yes and sent its team in two weeks before the wedding to cover all the activities leading up to the ceremony. Now the *Life* photographer and reporter were waiting, ready to record the moment as we exchanged our vows.

Six weeks later, in the May 18, 1953, issue, there it was. The five-page spread was headlined "*Life* goes to a schoolteacher's wedding and the pupils do all the work!"

For fifteen years the wedding and its nationwide coverage was the high point of our marriage. Sometimes one of us might say, only partially in jest, "From there it went straight downhill!" Our marriage didn't really plummet, but it surely did meander sadly through a downward spiral. We had what appeared to be a normal marriage, but underneath the facade neither of us was happy. We had lost any ability to communicate how we felt inside. Too often we kept our feelings to ourselves because of the danger that the other spouse would get upset or defensive if we expressed them. It was easier to avoid anything that might cause a problem.

Without realizing it, we were building a solid but invisible wall, brick by brick.

Dismantling that wall was not easy. Looking back on what we've been through, Florence and I sometimes marvel that we endured the challenges and the anguish involved in tearing it down. And sometimes we think about that ominous, overwhelming barrier and we wonder why it took us so long to see it. But we know now that we aren't the only husband and wife whose marriage has been divided by an invisible wall. As we travel around the world, sharing what we've learned, we see the same wall again and again. It can be built of many different kinds of bricks: misunderstanding, lack of communication, religious legalism, past emotional trauma, apathy, isolation. But whatever its components, this wall divides husbands and wives and keeps them from having the kind of loving, compassionate, thriving marriage God intended them to have.

How's *your* marriage? Have you and your wife built a wall that's keeping you from having the happy, fulfilling marriage God wants you to have? Could *your* wife write a letter like this one:

> Randall is very successful in his business, the vice president of an expanding, interstate company. He's been at the right place at the right time ever since he started with this firm twenty years ago. He's been given free rein to use his talents

and expertise, and I'm sure he feels very fulfilled in his accomplishments and efforts.

The second most important thing in his life seems to be sports. He has admitted a near obsession for sports and enjoys them all—football, baseball, basketball playoffs and championships, hockey, the Olympics. He reads every word of the newspaper's sports section every day, attends all the games he can, and frequently plays golf with clients.

It's good for a man to enjoy his work and enjoy sports. I know that. But I think this is also part of our problem: His job and his love of sports are so fulfilling he really doesn't feel a need to work on our marriage. His needs are basically met by his job and sports.

When he comes home he checks out emotionally. He goes upstairs to change his clothes for the evening, turns on the TV, and often doesn't come down until dinner is almost over. When he's home, the TV is always on.

He rarely does any sharing or communicating with me. When we do talk it's about routine household matters.

I'm beginning to believe he could live the rest of his life this way, functioning totally independently, doing his own thing, physically interacting in family matters but not displaying any feeling or affection toward me. I get the feeling Randall could live his life without anything I have to offer or contribute. Our relationship right now is very respectful but there is no depth or caring or affection. After sixteen years of marriage, snuggling or even touching in bed has ceased. Handholding, hugs, eye contact, and talking about *us* never happens.

Randall takes care of me and our two children's physical and financial needs 100 percent and more. He does the dishes every night and encourages me to pursue any interests or activities I enjoy. If you've got a man like this, how can you not feel guilty if you even think of complaining over the one area he lacks? Yet the more I try to convince myself how lucky I am, the more miserable I become!

I believe we are living in dysfunction (a word Randall strongly dislikes) because we are no longer emotionally bonding, we share no affection, and we are no longer a priority for each other.

Could this man possibly blow his perfect physical health because he shares nothing on a personal level with anyone?

Could he eventually have a stroke or a heart attack, or do so many people like him just live their whole lives like this? I believe marriage counseling may be the answer, but Randall doesn't want to go to counseling because he says we don't have a problem. He encourages me to get counseling if I need it, but he says he doesn't need it because the problem is all mine. He's perfectly content, but I'm miserable. Any insights you can give me as to what's normal or healthy and what I can expect will be greatly appreciated.

This letter, sent to us by an attractive Christian wife, describes many of the issues confronting couples today. Isn't it interesting that it was the wife who wrote to us, asking for insights or advice? The husband didn't. After all, he had no problems; he was happy and content with his life.

But was he really happy and content? At work, probably yes. At home? Even he must have felt the wall that had grown between him and his wife. He must have felt the detachment that had crept into his marriage.

What Does Your Future Look Like?

When couples come to us describing this kind of relationship and asking for our advice, we always ask them the same question: "Where will you be ten years from now?" Thinking about the possible answers to that scary question usually motivates couples to do something about where they are today.

Where will Randall be ten years from now? Will he be happier and more content? Or will he have retreated further and deeper into the shell he has created for himself? Will he have given up any hope for a life of peace, joy, and contentment? Most people do. Rather than face the issues and expend the effort required in repairing a troubled relationship, many have given up. They have lost any hope that things can be different, so they just go on living one miserable day after another.

Some have turned away. They have walked out or sought solace in a new relationship. This is almost never the best solution. We have never heard anyone say, "Let me tell you about my wonderful divorce."

Who Takes the First Step toward Help?

It is almost always women who take the first step toward resolving problems, seeking help, and finding answers. When Florence and I speak at couples' conferences, it is always fascinating to ask, "In how many of your homes was it the wife's idea to come here this weekend?" Invariably most of the women's hands go up. Then we ask, "How many of you men initiated the idea to come here tonight?" If any hands are raised at all, it is only one or two. Women always seem to take the first step. Why do we allow them to do this? Surely we want improvement just as much as they do!

This trend is also reflected in another question we ask groups of couples: "If it happened during your marriage, which one of you received the Lord first? Wives, if you were first, raise your hands." Invariably, 80 percent of the women's hands are raised. "Husbands, if you were first, raise your hands." A small number of hands go up.

It is the same in our home. Florence made that life-changing decision before I did. It was she who first began going back to church, to that evangelical congregation in North Haven, Connecticut. Then, in that same church about fifteen months later, I hesitatingly, but with conviction, raised my hand one Sunday morning to indicate that I, too, wanted to become a Christian.

In the same way, Florence took the first step again several years later when some deeply rooted problems in our marriage had to be addressed if we were to have any semblance of harmony and fulfillment in our relationship.

An interesting third example of this women-first phenomenon occurred recently as we were speaking at a weekend church conference in Columbus, Ohio. I had mentioned from the platform that there were some simple but very helpful handouts on our book table to assist couples with their communication—pink sheets for women, blue for men. Each listed twenty-five questions the spouses should answer separately. Then they would compare their responses and discuss their differences and their shared preferences and interests.[1]

Later in the day, as I was speaking to a break-out workshop with approximately twenty men and twenty women in it, I happened to ask, "How many of you have picked up a copy of the 'Communication Exercises for Husbands and Wives'?" Not a single man raised his hand, but most of the women did! Once again, this showed how women invariably take the first step when there is something to be gained that might help the relationship.

Why is this? Why do we men allow our women to be the first to seek improvement in our relationships? Why are we so blind to see the pain and the loneliness we cause our wives by our inability or unwillingness to express our feelings and to communicate with them on an emotional level?

Perhaps we are reluctant to expose ourselves, to acknowledge that we have any needs. We hesitate to let our feelings surface, thinking it is manly and virile to hide our pain, our disappointments, and even our guilt. Pride keeps us from sharing from our hearts. We tend to keep our feelings so bottled up that they only occasionally seep out—or explode uncontrollably. Then we feel all the more guilty and resolve never to make ourselves vulnerable again.

Even though we may refuse to acknowledge these feelings, our wives often know we have them. The truth is, our wives often know us far better than we know ourselves! They usually have a far greater grasp of the dynamics of our family and marriage than we do.

Accepting Full Responsibility as Provider and Protector

For years we men have willingly assumed our rightful role as provider and protector for our family. But we may have confined those responsibilities to the financial, physical, and in some cases spiritual aspects of our family and our marriage while totally ignoring the very important emotional aspects. Too often we abdicate to our wives the emotional nurturing of our relationship.

But isn't that part of the provider and protector's role too? Isn't it my role as a husband to protect my wife from emotional stress to the very best of my ability? This seems especially so when we understand that God has uniquely prepared us men to deal effectively with emotions, in many ways far better than women.

Then isn't it time we wake up to the needs of our families in those areas that we have traditionally neglected? Any man who has an unhappy wife for any reason has a problem. Isn't it time we take a stand and acknowledge that when this kind of problem exists in our relationships we may have been part of the cause? We cannot experience the very best God intends for us until we recognize this possibility and work—even becoming the initiator—to solve that problem.

I should know!

After fifteen years of marriage I had peace, or so I thought. I was content. I didn't know there was a problem. Therefore, I reasoned, if there *was* a problem in our home or our marriage it had to be Florence's fault. She was the one who needed help. Like Randall in the letter I shared previously, I, too, encouraged my wife to get counseling.

Yes, I was frustrated because I had an emotional wife—but my frustration was not caused by my worry over her unhappiness. Instead, I was frustrated because I felt Florence was so consumed with her own problems she didn't have time to recognize that my needs weren't being met!

She didn't seem to have time for me. But I simply resigned myself that this was how our life was going to be, assuming there would not be anything better.

Oh, how wrong I was!

2

TURNING POINTS

At first, Florence and I seemed to fit so well. We were very different, yes, but our strengths seemed to complement each other. I loved to do the things she was weak at—planning, scheduling, and organizing. I enjoyed putting things down on paper and charting them out. I liked to ponder things until I was satisfied they were just right.

In social relationships, self-confidence, and enthusiasm, Florence was a natural. Everyone loved her. People naturally gravitated toward her. I needed that in her. I knew I was not that kind of person. I remember telling my mother, when she asked me how I knew Florence was the right one for me, that we were like two complex cogs, rotating together. "We mesh perfectly together," I said. And in many ways we did.

And in many ways our relationship was doomed. One of those ways was in the unexpressed emotional baggage I carried with me into our marriage. I'll talk about that in later chapters and explain the damage it did and how I finally came to see and understand it. In this chapter, though, I want to share with you the first, basic discovery Florence and I made about our different personalities. This discovery became a simple tool that helped us restore our relationship to the kind of marriage God intended it to be.

When we were dating, we tended to focus on each other's strengths, the things that attracted and drew us together. In marriage, however, we soon turned our focus to those few weaknesses that, in the euphoria of courtship, we had overlooked.

I remember thinking during our dating days that Florence was 95 percent perfect, really all that anyone could expect. And that other 5 percent? Well, I had the rest of our lives together to help her with that. And wouldn't she want to be as perfect as she could be? What a shock it was to learn that Florence didn't enjoy and even began to resent my "helping" her with some of these little areas that could be improved. I needed a perfect and loving wife, but she didn't appreciate my helpful training.

Gradually the wall began to rise between us.

Scratching the Surface of Our Problems

I wanted to be the best husband I could be. I worked at becoming all that Florence desired. I am the kind of person who is called a perfectionist. I have always wanted to do everything to the best of my ability, never taking shortcuts. My theme has always been, If it's worth doing, it's worth doing right.

I had been raised in a pseudo-Christian religion that had taught me I was "God's perfect child." This background only served to confirm, since I was already perfect, that any problems had to be Florence's.

As the years went by I became more and more frustrated with Florence's apparent inability to understand me and to be the wife I needed. She just didn't seem to care about what was most important to me. I needed to be loved and appreciated, but it just wasn't happening. In fact, my deep hunger for love and appreciation only pushed her further away from me.

I didn't understand any of this. I just knew I was becoming more and more unhappy. I began to plunge into my work to forget the hurt I felt at home. I had no guidelines as to what was wrong and no frame of reference for what was right. I simply knew this was not what I needed or expected in marriage. Since I knew I was doing all I could do, it was very easy to feel the problems were all Florence's. *If only she would change,* I silently fumed. *If only she would become more warm and tender, more loving, we could be happy with each other.*

Obviously she needed help, and I encouraged her to try to find answers or go to someone who had some wisdom that could make her see what she needed to do to become a better wife.

One day she shared with her doctor some of her feelings and her hurts in our marriage, and he agreed to try to be a mediator and to meet with me. I met with him one time and found him to be a very pleasant and kindly man, gracious and caring. I enjoyed talking with him and was eager for his evaluation of our situation and for his recommendations. I couldn't wait for Florence to have her next appointment with him—so I was completely unprepared for the report she brought home. The only thing I remember is her comment that he felt I was "very immature." *Immature? Me?* I couldn't believe he could even say such a thing! It seemed too obvious that the problems were all hers. *She's the one who needs to change, to shape up, and he thinks I'm immature!* It was clear to me this doctor had no wisdom that could help us. I immediately wrote him off and concluded he should stick to obstetrics for he certainly had nothing our marriage needed. He couldn't even see the real problem! This ended our very short experience with marriage counseling.

I had no idea what the real problems were, so I had no idea how we could solve them. Because I was so busy building my business and trying to support my growing family, I never took the time to do what I now encourage all men to do: Read, study, and learn all you can about yourself, about marriage, about child-raising, about what a wife needs from a husband, what your differences are, and how to understand and meet each other's emotional needs.

Since I wasn't a Christian, I had no idea that the Bible had some very clear and specific directions for the husband and the wife, for the family. Looking back, I can honestly say I didn't even know help was available. The one time we tried it with the obstetrician, it seemed to be such a disaster we never looked any further. The fact was the doctor, despite his good intentions, was dealing in an area in which he had little experience. His statement to Florence about me was accurate but unfortunately insensitive. My immaturity was only the surface of our problems. We later discovered there was much more; the roots of our problems ran deep, deep into my past.

Times of Joy and Sorrow

By 1960, Florence and I had two healthy and beautiful little girls, Lauren and Marita, ages five and one. I loved my two daughters and did everything I knew to do to be the best father I could for them. I did my best to teach them and train them, to nurture them, and to love them. However, like many other young fathers—particularly us perfectionists— I also wanted to have a son, especially since I was building a food-service management business that someone would have to take over someday. In my immaturity I somehow thought businesses lasted forever and could only be run by men.

In 1961 our first son was born. I proudly gave him my name, fulfilling one of my ambitions since childhood, to sire Frederick J. Littauer III. He, too, was a beautiful child, and in many ways he looked like he would grow up to be just like his father. But when little Freddie was about six months old, he began to wake up screaming during the night. We all, even little Lauren, took turns holding him, rocking him, and trying to comfort him until at last he would quiet down and we could go back to bed.

Finally, when the screaming got unbearable—for Freddie as well as the rest of us—Florence took him to our pediatrician. We expected the doctor to diagnose some kind of minor illness that could be treated with drugs or household remedies. Instead, he told Florence bluntly, "This child is hopelessly brain damaged."

A specialist gave us the same, heartbreaking diagnosis. There was nothing we could do for him, the doctors said. All our willpower, the misplaced faith in healing inspired by my religious background, all the money in the world, would not help my little namesake. They recommended we put him in a private children's nursing home in northern Connecticut where he would receive the loving attention and care he needed. We did as they suggested.

After Freddie was diagnosed, the doctors advised us to have another child to replace our lost son. There was no known cause or explanation for the brain deterioration he was suffering, they said. It was not long before our second son was born, and Florence was determined that nothing would happen to this child. She chose a name related to her own: Laurence Chapman Littauer. Little Larry was carefully tested and examined at birth to make certain he was completely healthy. The report was 100 percent positive. We rejoiced. We finally had a healthy replacement for our little Freddie, still in that children's home, by now blind, deaf, and without any human faculties.

Little Larry developed normally, and we became a family in recovery. On February 14, exactly six months after Larry's birth, we received a call from the nursing home telling us his older brother, now two years old, had strangled and died in the night. We had many emotions to deal with, including grief and loss. And we struggled with the question some friends and relatives had raised: "Should we have kept him home with us?" But there was also a sense of relief that this chapter of our life was now behind us.

One week later Florence went into little Larry's room and, as she frequently did, waved her hand across his face. No response. She tapped her hand on the crib rail. He was awake, but there was no response. She picked him up, shook him gently, and cried, "Smile, Larry, smile!" But Larry didn't smile.

Emotions poured over her as she recognized the same lack of reactions she had seen in Freddie. Quickly she wrapped him up and took him right in to see the same doctor who had examined Freddie. She says she will never forget the look on the doctor's face. After a brief examination he told her quietly, "Florence, I'm sure it's the same thing."

Both Florence and I were in shock. How could this have happened a second time? Our two daughters were perfectly normal and healthy. Why not our two sons? What was wrong? Once again there were no answers. This time, however, we took Larry to the Metabolic Research Unit of Johns Hopkins Hospital in Baltimore to have a brain biopsy done. Once again the answer came back: There is no hope. The biopsy indicated Larry did not have a normal brain, just a small, smooth, round ball. The doctors told us he would never live beyond five years of age. I brought him home on the plane, his little head swathed in bandages. From that day on he was no more than a living vegetable. He could not hear or see, and soon he had no responses whatsoever. Once again, we had to make a decision. Keeping little Larry at home was much too traumatic for Florence and also for our two little girls. And it was not easy on me.

I will never forget the day we bundled little Larry up and drove him to northern Connecticut to that same children's home where his brother had died just a few months before. That was the last time Florence ever saw him, but I continued to visit him periodically, even after we moved to California in 1968.

I will never forget one of those visits. I had flown in to Connecticut from California on a business trip. On Saturday afternoon I was in the Hartford area and had some time available. So I decided to make the two-hour drive through the beautiful but rugged northern Connecticut countryside to visit my son. One might wonder why I would go to visit him. After all, he could not see or hear. He probably could not even sense I was there. Even though he was older, he was still tiny. He had never grown.

When I arrived at this large, white converted home there was nobody in the front reception area. I turned to the large room on the right, which might have once been the dining room. There were many cribs in that room, and on the door frame was a list of the names of the little children there, all pitiful examples of something gone awry. I looked in vain on the list for my son's name. He had been in that room the last time I had been here, about a year before. I walked to the big room on the left side of the house. Larry's name was not on that list either. But inside the room I saw an attendant feeding a child about the size of a seven-year-old. The girl's body looked normal but her head was a fraction of normal size. I walked over to this kindly woman, wondering how anyone could work in a place such as this, probably with very low pay and rarely any thanks. It must take a special calling, I decided, feeling grateful there were people who felt called to do such work and who could handle the emotions.

In a very halting voice I said, "Excuse me, but I'm looking for my son. His name is Larry Littauer."

"Oh yes," was her sweet and gentle reply. "I know where he is. Please come with me." She led me back to the stairs. On the second floor we passed through one room with three or four cribs in it and headed into another room. There she pointed to a little child in worn, hand-me-down clothes lying on a cushion on the floor. Then she left the room so I could visit with my son, the child on the cushion. Visit with him? How does one visit with someone who is blind and deaf and doesn't even know you are there? I had driven two hours to see my little son and I couldn't "visit" with him. He was now about sixteen years old but still the same size he had been when we took him there when he was one.

All I could do was to stand over him and weep and pray. I said, "Thank You, Lord, for my little son Larry." As I continued to stand over him and to talk to my Father about my son, I prayed, "Lord, take him home, for his life is so wasted." Instantly I heard a response, a message I have never forgotten. It probably was the first time I had heard this voice speak to me. Clearly in my head I heard, "His life is no more wasted than is your life when you're not serving Me, no more wasted than the life of any Christian who just sits in church on Sunday morning." Without question I knew who had spoken to me.

As I drove away from the nursing home that Saturday afternoon, those words kept ringing in my mind. Now I knew why I had been led to drive that long distance to visit a son who would not even know I was there. My Father in heaven had a message He wanted me to hear. He needed me to be there. He wanted me to cry out to Him.

So instead of leaving my son feeling depressed and discouraged, I had a joy and exuberance in my soul as I headed south to spend the night with my brother and his family in Westport. Over and over again God's words came to me: *His life is no more wasted than is your life when you're not serving Me, no more wasted than the life of any Christian who just sits in church on Sunday morning.*

I was scheduled to speak that next Sunday morning in my brother's church in Wilton. The message I shared was that message the Lord had given me the day before. The doctors in Baltimore had told us Larry would not live longer than about five years. But they were wrong. Larry died when he was nineteen years old, still the same size he had been when we had taken him to the nursing home when he was one.

Real Life beneath the Happy Facade

As a dear Christian friend once pointed out to us, both Freddie and Larry, in a very real sense, gave their lives that we might find life. This is true because it was during that memorable visit to see Larry that I first heard God's voice speaking directly to me. And it was in 1965, after Freddie had died, that Florence finally, reluctantly agreed to go to a Christian Women's Club meeting. There she heard—really heard—the gospel for the first time. Agreeing that she needed help, she asked the Lord Jesus to give her a new life.

Several months later, in God's sovereign timing, a young pastor came to our door and invited Florence to come to his church. She took the girls and went the very next day, only to find that it met in the gymnasium of an elementary school. Hardly the kind of church she had envisioned for her daughters to be married in someday! On the following Sunday, at the urging of my two daughters, I went as well. As a family we quickly became faithful regulars of the Evangelical Baptist Church in North Haven, Connecticut. After attending this church consistently for twelve months, I responded to the call of the Savior, raising my hand during the invitation one Sunday morning in August 1966. During those moments I heard the pastor say four times to others in the congregation, "I see your hand." He waited and then asked again, "Anyone else?" I could wait no longer. I knew that I, too, needed a change in my life. If Jesus offered hope, this was where I needed to be. I raised my hand.

Afterward the pastor asked the five of us who had raised our hands to come forward and be welcomed into the family of God. I watched as four teenage girls left their seats and walked forward. But this thirty-seven-year-old husband and father could not move. I was glued to my chair! After the service was over I went up to the pastor to tell him my commitment was sincere and I meant it, but I was simply not able to come forward as the others had.

I didn't understand it then, but I was making my first contact with the pride barrier that so often keeps men from doing what they *want* to do and know they *should* do. We are different from women, and sometimes this difference is decidedly not to our advantage. Frankly, I was a chicken about anything that touched on the emotional. I didn't want to reveal what I was really feeling inside. I have learned this is typical with men.

As I look back on my first year as a Christian, I recognize it as one of the most difficult periods of my life. It would be nice to be able to say that once I had Christ in my life, all my problems and issues disappeared. Quite the contrary, things became much more difficult! My relationship with Florence took a new low turn. We had already rejected any thought of divorce, realizing our two daughters had already been through too much trauma in having two baby brothers taken out of the home, never to be seen again. In removing our baby boys to what was a better place for them, we thought we were sparing our girls pain by relieving them from having to see the suffering infants every day. Much, much later we learned that, despite our good intentions, we actually created a new issue for them to face. They received a subconscious message that if they weren't "good" the same thing might happen to them: They, too, would be sent away and "abandoned." In their young minds, what they could understand was that if they cried too much, as their brothers had done throughout the night, the same thing would happen to them. After all, they had seen it happen to both of their brothers!

Oblivious to these unspoken messages we, as young parents in pain, did the best we knew to maintain a semblance of healthy family life. But beneath the happy facade, our relationship deteriorated. We did not even begin to understand the dynamics that were pulling us apart. We both knew we were unhappy and unfulfilled, but we didn't know what to do about it.

We had already tried everything we knew. I had tried to remake Florence into the kind of wife I needed and, in a sense, I had succeeded in remaking her. She learned to subjugate all her natural personality in order to try to please me and to cope with what was becoming more and more evident: my very critical spirit and suppressed anger. In doing so she put on a "personality mask" and lost all her natural joy and sparkle. She had changed to try to please me, but I was unhappy with the new wife I had created. She was no longer the girl I had married. Instead of exhibiting her own God-given and natural strengths, she was functioning in her weaknesses.

Who could help us? We knew of no one. We could only do our best on our own. We were not very successful, but we never gave up. I began to study and enjoy Scripture for the first time in my life, and I began to find truth that applied to me. I made every effort to conform my life, my feelings, and my attitudes to what God wanted me to be. But later I would learn I was merely applying "scriptural band-aids" to my deep, smoldering pain.

A Life-Changing Milestone

In January 1968 Florence and I flew out to California to attend a laymen's conference at Campus Crusade for Christ in San Bernardino. This turned out to be a milestone in our lives for several reasons. We took giant steps forward in our Christian life as we began to understand more about what the Spirit-filled life means. We learned how to readily and comfortably share our faith.

And I learned they needed help in the kitchen. Four out of the five nights we were there they served fried chicken! For one who had been in the restaurant and food-service management business for many years, this made no sense at all. Their obvious need for help in the kitchen was to become quite significant for us in the very near future, as I'll explain a little later.

But probably the most important thing that happened to us occurred the day before we left. As we were browsing in the Campus Crusade Bookstore, Dr. Ron Jones, one of the staff members, handed us a book and said, "Here's a book you need to read." It was Tim LaHaye's *Spirit-Controlled Temperament*. I wondered, *What has he learned about me during these four days to know that I needed this book?* Had Ron already observed that I was not Spirit-controlled? Had he perceived problems in me that needed immediate attention? Gratefully, but with some trepidation, we accepted his generous offer. In doing so, we set out on a journey that would change our lives. This one book was to open a vast new vista for our marriage and our ministry in the years to come.

Florence and I plunged into the book on the way home and quickly learned an amazing new truth: We were both created with very different personalities or temperaments. That meant we both had very different strengths and weaknesses. And it meant that *different* does not mean *wrong!* We finally realized our many years trying to change each other had been misguided, unintentionally harmful—and futile. Florence had tried to get me to have a sense of humor and be more spontaneous, more able to accept things that had not been planned in advance, while I had been trying to get her to become more punctual, schedule-conscious, and organized. I had been trying to make her more like me, and she had been trying to make me more like her! As a result, over the years we had both become disenchanted and frustrated with each other.

Now, for the first time, we found out that God had intentionally given us different personalities. As we studied and learned about the personalities we could easily see that my strengths filled in the gaps of Florence's

weaknesses and that her strengths perfectly complemented my weaknesses. (This, in itself, was quite revealing since it was probably the first
time I even realized I had any weaknesses!)

Thus occurred the second important breakthrough in my life, the first
being the day a year and a half earlier when I had committed my life to the
Lord. Now we had tools that could help us understand each other, and
even better, perhaps, understand what we were doing to each other.

Florence loves to tell the story of what happened next. One Saturday
night we invited a number of couples from our church to come over to
learn about the four basic personality types. We had only been home
from California a few weeks and had barely finished reading the book.
But that didn't stop Florence from wanting to have a party and teach
others what we had learned. Everyone had a good time, and under
Florence's humorous sharing they began to see each other for the first
time in a new light. At the end they asked, "Couldn't we do this again?"
Never one to turn down an opportunity for a gathering, Florence quickly
agreed.

Before our guests arrived for the second session, I (naturally) made a
chart of ten of the strengths and weaknesses of each of the four personalities. I thought we needed to be a little bit better organized about this
whole thing than we had at our impromptu first session. As part of the
second night's activity I planned to break up the nine couples into groups
based on the personality they felt they most closely identified with. Florence was to be the leader of the Sanguines. I would be the leader of the
Melancholies, and one other husband was to be lead the Phlegmatics.
We didn't seem to have any Cholerics that night; apparently they were
all out running some other more significant activities. (I'll summarize the
characteristics of these personality types in chapter 5, but if you'd like
to study them in detail, I recommend Florence's books, *Your Personality
Tree*, *Personality Plus*, and *Personality Puzzle*.)

Florence and the noisy Sanguines headed off to our bedroom, the
farthest point from the rest of the house, with the assignment to go
through the ten-point lists of strengths and weaknesses and see how these
characteristics applied to them. I stayed in the living room with the
Melancholies, and the Phlegmatic group was sent into the family room
and settled onto the couches. We each had one hour to complete our assignment. I watched the clock and paced our group so we would finish
exactly on time. I decided it had been a good idea to send the Sanguines
as far away as possible. Even in their far-off room they were awfully noisy
and disruptive! They were having too much fun, I thought, and were
probably not being serious enough about the assignment.

Sure enough, at the end of our sixty minutes I went in to check on Florence and the Sanguines and they were roaring with laughter when I opened the door. I asked, "How far have you gotten with the list?"

"We're still on point one, 'talkative,'" Florence said with a bright smile. "We've had so much fun, we never got past the first point! Is our time up already?" I was so disappointed with their lack of self-discipline. They had literally wasted the whole hour, just talking!

Then I went into the family room to see how the Phlegmatics had done with their lists. I could not believe what I saw. All five of them were sprawled out—you guessed it—*asleep on the couches!* I roused the one in charge to ask, "What did you do with the list?"

He stirred himself to groggily answer, "I read down the list and everyone said, 'uh-huh, uh-huh, uh-huh.' Since there was nothing else to do we just dozed off 'til you were all done."

If you're familiar with the personality types, you'll realize what we learned that night: These personality profiles do work. Each of our groups was amazingly true to form. Since that first experience, Florence and I have continued to study the personalities. For twenty-five years we have done comprehensive research and investigation and have used what we learned to help other couples see their differences and often the roots of their inability to communicate or to understand each other. We have taught this subject in seminars and conferences on three continents. It is the foundation, or an integral part of, at least half of the twenty-one books Florence has written. Yet it is the simplest tool we know of to help people begin to look at themselves, see why they function and think as they do, and understand others by understanding themselves.

Recently, when we were on Don Hawkins's nationally broadcast radio program, "Life Perspectives," we were talking about stress. We were explaining how to identify the sources so stressed-out people can take steps to correct or change it; this is one of the self-analysis sections of our book, *Get a Life Without the Strife* (Thomas Nelson, 1993). But instead of asking about stress problems the first listener to call in wanted to thank us for our books on the personalities. She said her and her husband's understanding of their differences had taken much of the stress out of their marriage.

Becoming the Man God Wants You to Be

When we men are willing to take a look at who we are and why we act the way we do, we will take a giant stride toward solving our own frustrations and then to becoming the men, the husbands, and the fathers

God wants us to be. He calls us to be the head of the wife. But how can we be what we know we should be and what we want to be when our heads are in the sand about ourselves, our hurts, and our disappointments?

Today Florence and I experience the relationship God intended for a husband and wife. We are now ONE in every sense of the word. Today I am completely fulfilled as a man and a husband. And my wife is free of all the stress that once filled her. I know now that I was the cause of much of that stress, but I would never have guessed it back then.

How did I do it? That's what I want to share with you in the chapters ahead so that you, too, can have the kind of thriving, fulfilling marriage we've found.

3

I WAS BLIND
BUT NOW I SEE

When I walked out of that wedding ceremony in 1953 with Florence on my arm, I carried, unbeknownst to me or anyone else in that packed sanctuary, an old, invisible, banged-up suitcase filled with dirty emotional laundry. On its side was a big, ugly sign that said REJECTION.

The main reason I had wanted to get married was to have someone to love me. Of course I had never analyzed my feelings, never checked to see if this was a healthy and valid reason to get married at all. I never even wondered if I was emotionally healthy. I just wanted so desperately to have someone I could depend on, someone who would be mine. Someone who would fill forever that huge gap inside me where love was supposed to go. That gap would cause a big problem for me—and my family—in the years ahead.

In the last chapter, I shared with you how Florence and I overcame many of our problems by learning to use our understanding of the personality types to restore our relationship. This tool has had a profound effect on making our marriage and our ministry thriving, fulfilling components of our lives together. But there was still that other problem that had to be overcome. Before I could be the kind of husband and father—the kind of *man*—God intended me to be, I had to unlock that old, invisible suitcase I'd been carrying around all those years and empty all the hurtful, maddening, unexpressed feelings of rejection it held.

But for many years I didn't even know the suitcase was there. I was blind to the emotional hurts inside me—and to the emotional pain I was causing the ones I loved most. I was blind. But at last I began to see. Here's how it began:

Life before the Crash

As I mentioned in the previous chapter, in January 1968 Florence and I had gone to California to attend a laymen's conference at Campus Crusade for Christ in San Bernardino. When I discovered the turmoil that plagued the program's kitchen, I offered to come back and use my professional expertise and experience to straighten out the problem. On Memorial Day 1968 we returned and found a disaster waiting to happen. In two weeks Crusade's busy summer program would begin, bringing an average of twelve hundred college students each week for training. Each of those twelve hundred students would be fed three meals per day.

In addition Crusade for Christ was just finishing construction of a major new housing and dining facility. It was on the same campus as the other buildings but was remote from the "hotel," the main structure that housed the existing guest rooms, dining rooms, and kitchen.

I quickly realized that serving and dishwashing areas had been built in the new facility, but no areas or equipment had been set aside for food preparation. This meant all the food to be served at each meal had to be prepared in the hotel kitchen and hauled to the new area. Then the shipping containers would have to be sent back to the hotel with the leftovers.

I also learned that the local health department had closed the entire kitchen during the previous summer's program and food had to be trucked in from Los Angeles by a caterer.

This was clearly going to be a very complex project, and no one on the staff had the experience to make it work smoothly. To complicate things even more, another seventy-five college students were coming in to work without pay as "summer staff" in the kitchen and food service. True, they were motivated, but they were totally without experience.

It didn't take long to formulate my recommendation: "Get out of the food-service business as quickly as possible and stick to what you do well, training college students in Christian evangelism." But the leaders had already thought of this. They told me they had talked to local catering companies, and the companies were not interested in providing any of these services. Crusade seemed to be headed for big trouble—again.

There seemed to be no simple solution. As a friend of the ministry, I offered to take over the food service, just for the summer, through my New England-based company. I promptly prepared a simple contract through which I assumed all the responsibilities of the food service, locking myself into a very low price per meal. Crusade could save a great deal of money over what it had spent the previous summer, and I could only lose if I failed to deliver according to the contracted price.

Since we had just come for the weekend, Florence and I flew back home to the East Coast, where I repacked enough clothes to last two weeks. My plan was to go back out west and get things organized, then bring out one of our college food-service managers from Connecticut whose program was just closing down for the summer. He was excited about the chance to come to California and work for the summer, and I was glad to see him when he finally arrived. We were already in the thick of it by then. After another two weeks I called Florence back in Connecticut and said, "Honey, you and the children better pack up and come out here. This thing is even bigger than I imagined. I doubt that I will get out of here all summer."

They promptly flew out to California. Our two girls and our adopted son Freddie were excited about spending the summer in California. We lived in the hotel, where the children swam in the pools and met new friends while Dad worked in the kitchen twelve to fifteen hours a day, seven days a week. Florence was able to go to many of the lectures and seminars, and was even asked to speak once or twice. One of her messages on Christian hospitality was a highlight of the two-week staff training.

In a very short time the food service was functioning smoothly. Everyone who had been there the previous summer was amazed at the difference. When I found that we were running under budget, we even added sirloin steak once a week. Things were really going well, and within a few weeks I was asked to consider joining the full-time staff to replace the hotel manager, who had submitted his resignation, effective September 1. This meant selling our home and giving up everything we had worked so hard to build in Connecticut and moving permanently to California.

I prayed and meditated and discussed it with Florence for a solid week. We had no clear sense of direction until one Saturday morning I took out a yellow legal pad and made a chart of the various pros and cons for both California and Connecticut. All of a sudden it hit me there was no sacrifice in staying where we were, in our "comfort zone" in Connecticut. Everything that was convenient and comfortable for us was there. Everything that was uncertain and sacrificial for us was in California. Florence agreed with me. The whole concept had a sound of excitement that appealed to her Sanguine personality. With this agreement and confirmation, I told Crusade, "Yes, we will come."

As part of our acceptance process to join the staff we had to take some psychological tests and then meet with the psychologist. Neither of us will ever forget his observation about Florence. He told her, "You have a very rebellious attitude." We both vehemently denied his conclusions. I even told him Florence was always very agreeable to everything I wanted to do. But he insisted this spirit was there. Fortunately, it didn't keep us from being accepted, apparently because we were needed. I felt a little smug. The psychologist had made no negative comments about me. This confirmed my feelings that any problems in our marriage were hers.

It was not until years later when we started working with people's emotions that we realized how right he was. However, his tests had failed to identify *why* she had a rebellious spirit. Now we know the reason: Florence was wearing a mask of compliance and dutiful obedience as a coping mechanism. It was the only way she could survive. We both had strong personalities, but I was the more demanding and insistent one. Whenever Florence didn't agree with my position or a decision I wanted to make, I always threw out a hundred different reasons from my masculine and melancholy perspectives why my position was rationally better. Too often I failed to hear her feminine intuition that something just didn't feel right. I wore her down with my logic until she agreed. In this way I was able to feel we had made the decision together and were of one mind when, in fact, she had simply caved in.

Florence had also learned that if she didn't cave in, she would be subjected to my repressed anger, an anger I didn't even know I had. Nevertheless I used this anger to control her without even being aware of what I was doing.

Over the years of our marriage Florence had learned to become compliant and agreeable, but hidden underneath was this rebellious spirit. Now, with the insight I've gained over the last few years, I take full responsibility for suppressing Florence's natural, healthy spirit throughout the first three and a half decades of our marriage. But back then it would be a long time before I realized that I was the one with the problems, not Florence. She had all she could do to try to keep our family together and to keep her own emotions healthy. It is no wonder that a submerged, rebellious spirit developed inside her without either of us being aware of it.

We remained on the Campus Crusade staff for one year but lived on the grounds a second year until we moved into a new home in San Bernardino. We had completely removed ourselves from Connecticut although the business I had started there was still operating. In time I was able to sell that food-service business and start a new business in California, a chain of auto-repair shops. I remained in that business for about twelve years, eventually turning it over to our son Fred to own and operate.

Those years were filled with financial struggle. We ate, we lived, and somehow we survived. But at one point we had to sell our home and move into a much smaller condominium because I needed the equity in our home to settle financial obligations I had incurred in the business. All this was a tremendous strain for Florence. At the time I could not relate to her concerns and emotions over these struggles. I was the one, I thought, who was carrying all the burden. I was the one who was working all the hours. I was the one who somehow had to meet the payroll every week.

I never complained to her. All I wanted from her was her support, her understanding of what I was facing each day, and her unconditional love for me. Despite all these stresses in our life, I generally slept soundly each night while Florence seemed to toss and toss. In my naiveté, I attributed her inability to cope with her lack of faith. This was one more way I was able to cast all the blame and responsibility on her.

She, on the other hand, felt I was out of touch with reality and tended to spiritualize everything. Once again, we both did the best we could under very adverse circumstances over which we seemed to have no control. With these financial, emotional, and spiritual stresses in our lives we had to work hard to keep any semblance of togetherness. We worked at trying to build a love relationship based on scriptural principles.

I spent hours searching the Scriptures, trying to find ways to cement and strengthen my relationship with my heavenly Father. I knew if I was right with God I could eventually have the relationship with Florence I had always wanted. I wanted so much to be the man, the husband, and the father God wanted me to be. I thought we were making slow but steady progress to achieving the harmony and love we ought to be able to experience.

By September 1983 Florence had become a popular and successful author and speaker, and we made a conscious decision to always travel together on Florence's speaking events. We felt it was important to maintain a clear public profile by being seen together. We were too often mistaken for other Christian speakers who were falling, and there were even occasional rumors that we were drifting apart as well. But nothing could have been further from the truth. Things were not perfect, by any means, but we were both working diligently to improve all that we could.

Then my world came crashing down . . .

Discovering the Source of My Hurts

In 1987 Florence and I sponsored a seven-day Christian cruise to Alaska. I had initiated, planned, and promoted the entire event; we agreed that I would be in charge. Altogether, we would be taking some sixty people with us, including our daughter Marita and Lana Bateman, a friend from Dallas who has a healing prayer ministry. Our program aboard the *Cunard Princess* was to include several seminar sessions.

The first hint of trouble occurred when we sat down to review our individual workshop assignments. When Florence asked me if there was a topic I wanted to speak on I included "How to Meet Your Mate's Emotional Needs," a subject I had presented a few times in other settings with positive results.

Florence looked me right in the eye and said, "You can't teach something you haven't learned to do yourself."

I was stunned, dumbfounded, knocked speechless by this unexpected blow. My mind was in chaos as I struggled to respond, but I couldn't say a word. All I could do was wonder, *What is she talking about? We've made a lot of progress, and I think I've even made more than she has. Haven't we been getting along? Everything seems OK to me. What on earth does she mean?*

I had questions, but I couldn't get them out. I just sat there silently; I shrugged, brushed aside her comment, and offered instead to leave the speaking to her and the other leaders while I tended to the physical arrangements.

But inside I hurt. Oh, how I hurt! And as the cruise continued my misery deepened, although I tried to hide it from everyone else as I arranged the chairs for the workshops and made sure everyone's accommodations were satisfactory. After all, I was in charge, the host of the cruise. I had to make sure my guests were having a good time, even if I wasn't. So despite my growing emotional turmoil I showed nothing but cheer and peace on the outside—or so I thought.

In my misery I became more and more withdrawn from Florence. But she hardly seemed to notice until the last afternoon of the cruise. Then she sought me out and said she needed to talk with me—in our cabin. When I arrived I was amazed to find Marita and Lana there too.

In that cramped little cabin my life changed forever, and it certainly wasn't a painless evolution. In fact it was one of the most agonizing times of my life.

Florence told me I had a lot of anger inside me, and that I needed to do something about it because she couldn't live with it any longer.

Again I was shocked, but again I kept my composure. I automatically started rationalizing how she was wrong. *I* wasn't the one with the problem;

I wasn't angry. I had been wronged by her statement during the planning session and now, instead of apologizing she was continuing to attack me! How could she think I had anger inside me? I'd never hit her, never exploded at her, never even yelled at her, at least not that I could recall.

Then the three of them—Florence, Marita, and Lana—took turns telling me I was in denial. They said I was denying who I really was—an anger-filled man.

In my book *The Promise of Healing*, I describe what happened next:

> What was happening here? This was unbelievable!
>
> The more I thought about . . . how unfair and ridiculous it was—three against one—I began to boil inside. I could feel it coming up. I was getting mad. I was angry!
>
> Angry?
>
> Yes, I was angry. Was it possible? Could they be right? Was it true that there was anger in me? As these thoughts raced through my mind, I tried to grasp what was being said.
>
> Suddenly, a calm came over me. Instantly I knew what it was. It was the Holy Spirit quieting my shattered emotions. I became willing to listen. I became willing to hear what they were telling me. I heard myself say, "All right, if you see anger in me, I am willing to go to someone who can help me." I would never have believed I'd say those words. I never thought I needed counseling. I had thought it was Florence who needed help, but here I was agreeing to go.[1]

By confronting me Florence took a big chance, risking everything—her whole ministry, her Christian reputation, and everything we had achieved together. She did it because she was not willing to settle for *good* when *better* was available.

There was no way she could predict my reaction or response. She simply had to trust the results to the Lord. She had spent much time in prayer and in counsel with many wise counselors, knowing "in the multitude of counselors there is safety" (Prov. 11:14). This confrontation was, without a doubt, the most emotionally painful experience I have ever had. But as awful as it was for me, there is now no doubt in my mind that it was essential. There was surely no other way Florence could have gotten my attention and broken through the wall of denial I had built around myself. This was the only way she could get me to see in myself what was already quite clear to her and to others. They knew I needed help. I was the only one who didn't know it.

Suddenly the snug, safe, little world I had built for my feelings came crashing down on me. I found out there were things within me—hurt, fear, and most of all, anger—that pushed people away. And one of those people was my wife, the very one I craved to have emotionally close to me. I finally saw that it was I who needed to change. I was the one who needed cleansing and healing, not my wife.

When I admitted that I had a problem and agreed to go to someone for counseling, Florence already had that someone in mind.

In December 1987 I was in intensive counseling four hours a day for two and a half weeks. Finally, with this caring professional's help, I could express feelings I had suppressed for years. I learned the feelings that had developed during my childhood were destructively affecting my adult attitudes and behavior. I also learned that feelings and emotions are God-given; they are not wrong, but they can be inappropriately expressed.

Finally I could open up that invisible suitcase of emotional hurts I'd been carrying around so long. I could realize that as a child, I had never felt loved or valued. I had known, intellectually, that my parents loved me. They always worked hard to provide for my brothers, my sister, and me. *But I never felt loved,* and I had carried this deep, empty chasm into my marriage. I expected Florence to cheerfully and continually spend her days filling what proved to be a bottomless pit. Needless to say, Florence had soon tired of this game. But when she pulled back emotionally, I again felt unloved. These emotions, which I later learned are feelings of rejection, triggered deep hurts and resentments from my childhood that I didn't even know existed. Then the hurts became frustrations, and the frustrations became anger.

Yes, finally I could see it, acknowledge it. The anger was there, and knowing where it came from gave me the ability to deal with it.

I have since learned that almost everyone is a victim of rejection to some degree. Psychologists describe rejection as the emotion resulting from the failure of parenting to provide the natural and necessary nurturing that is each child's birthright. Rejection affects people differently, and several members of the same family will respond to it in different ways due to their varying ages, personalities, and experiences.

Finding the Peace of God

The counseling I received was helpful, but it did not even begin to tap into the much deeper issues in my life that I was to discover two years later. When I left the counselor's office after the two and a half weeks, he gave me the name of another therapist closer to our home and urged me to call him. He felt strongly that I would need another two years of weekly therapy. What he did not know, or did not seem to understand, was that I was already going to THE Counselor, the one described in Isaiah 9:6: "And His Name shall be called Wonderful, Counselor, The mighty God, The everlasting Father, The Prince of Peace." I had been meeting with Him daily since August of that year, when He had started what would prove to be an amazing cleansing and healing process in my life.

This process had begun after breakfast on a Tuesday morning, August 18, 1987, in our vacation cabin on Little Sebago Lake in Maine. That's when I began a practice I have continued to the present day and hope I will never cease. I'll tell you more about it in chapter 16. But for now just let me say that I was directed by the Lord to try a new way of praying, and it changed my life. I had always struggled with prayer. Before that morning I had never been able to pray for more than two or three minutes. My mind would wander, or I would simply doze off. Obviously, my "old" kind of prayer had never been very meaningful for me. As a result, I spent very little time in prayer. But on that day in Maine I prayed earnestly and joyfully for an hour and twenty minutes!

I have since learned that I was not unique in finding it hard to pray. These problems of wandering thoughts, easy distractions, and overwhelming drowsiness are common for many Christians, particularly for those who have had childhood experiences similar to mine.

But that first day of my new way of praying made such a difference! I experienced the presence of God in such a way that it literally has changed my life. I found I was doing just what the Lord suggested in Matthew 11:28: "Come unto me, all ye that labor and are heavy laden, and I will give you rest."

Clearly I had labored. I'd worked hard to survive a roller-coaster business career, I'd endured endless financial stress, and now I had learned there was within me a lot of repressed anger. I was also "heavy laden" with the burden of an unsatisfying marriage. Jesus saw my labor. He understood that I felt heavy laden. And He promised me rest and inner peace. Since that morning in Maine I have diligently come to Him each day in prayer—genuine, effective, heartfelt prayer. I have done my part, and He has done more than His part. He has rescued my life and restored my relationship with my wife. My purpose for living has dramatically changed as a result of my daily coming to The Counselor.

Take Off the Blinders

Looking back, I sometimes ask myself if I wasted those first thirty-four years of my marriage. In many respects the answer has to be yes. There were many positive aspects of my life and our marriage during that period.

It wasn't all negative. But when compared with where we are today and what we have learned, the contrast with the past is almost inconceivable. Now if there is one desire for the remaining years of my life, it is to help others who are hurting to find the healing that is available to them, to give them hope that they can change, to open the eyes of those who have been blind to the joy that's possible for them.

I once was blind but now I see.

I see that I wrongly put all the blame for the difficulties in our marriage on Florence.

I see that the real problems were in me, not in her.

I see that because of the deep needs and hurts within me I manipulated her to continually fill the bottomless pit of my empty chasm.

I see that I almost destroyed the spontaneity and personality of my wife by my moods and critical spirit.

I see that I put the same pressures on my children as they were growing up that my parents put on me.

I see that my whole family had to dance around my emotions, never sure of how I would react.

I see why I took those unhealthy risks in business, many of which I then had to spend years paying for.

I see why I was never able to listen to others' advice, always thinking I knew better.

Now I understand why some people were afraid of me, why I have made so many poor choices in life, and why I had never known real happiness.

And I've learned that I was not alone in thinking that changes in the home depended on changes in the wife.

What is it about us men that makes us always seem to think we are perfect, that we don't need to change, that all the problems in our marriage relationship, or certainly the major ones, are our wives' fault? Why are we so reluctant to go to an objective third party for guidance or counseling? It would be a very rare experience for any pastor or counselor to have a husband come into the office and say, "My marriage is in trouble. What can you do to help me be the husband my wife needs?" If a husband *were* the first to come in, he would probably say, "My marriage is in trouble. My wife doesn't understand me; she isn't meeting my needs. Would you be willing to meet with her? Perhaps you can make her see what a husband needs from a wife."

If you have already been in counseling and quit after a while because you didn't like what the counselor said, or if you told your wife she should continue going but you didn't need it, you have done exactly what I did.

And you have done the same as most men who enter into any form of guidance to resolve marital issues.

Remember the letter in chapter 1 from Randall's wife? She wrote, "I believe marriage counseling may be the answer, but Randall doesn't want to go to counseling because he says we don't have a problem. He encourages me to get counseling if I need it, but he says he doesn't need it because the problem is all mine."

The same thing was expressed in a letter another woman wrote to us after reading our book, *Freeing Your Mind from Memories That Bind*. She wrote:

> Our marriage has been mostly sliding downhill. We have been to two different marriage counselors without ever getting any help at all. My husband has had at least two affairs, probably more. He's admitted them but never even apologized. Frankly, I don't think he even believes he did anything wrong. Instead he puts all the blame on me.
>
> He says our communication is rotten. But every time I try to talk to him, he blows up or walks out of the room. It's gotten to the point I don't dare open my mouth.
>
> He wants me to change. He doesn't think anything is his fault. He knows I have some problems that stem from my childhood, but he tells me to just put it all behind me, to stop living in the past. I don't think he wants to try to understand.
>
> We're like two singles living in the same house, and I'm beginning to wonder if it's worth it. If it weren't for the two children and financial reasons I'd leave him in a minute. Do I deserve this? Is there nothing better for me, a Christian, than to live like this for the rest of my life?

My own story follows the same pattern as this husband's behavior. Do you see any similarity in your own feelings and situation? If you do, you're not alone. Unfortunately, though, men almost never discuss this kind of thing; we rarely share our real hurts and frustrations with each other, with our wives, or with anyone else. As a result we aren't aware that most other men are struggling with the very same or similar problems at home. We may complain to one another occasionally, but we don't honestly share our feelings. How many men do you know who are in a support or sharing group where they frankly and openly express feelings and needs to encourage and learn from each other?

I ask this question expecting most men to answer none. I would have answered the same way ten years ago. I couldn't have expressed my own frustrations and probably didn't know a man who could. I wouldn't have been willing to openly expose my needs to anyone I thought I would ever see again. The only way most of us would allow ourselves to be vulnerable would be within a group of strangers when we knew we would never have to face them again. Perhaps at an out-of-state men's retreat. But in a group from our church? Never.

If there had been a book like this ten or fifteen years ago, would I have read it? Probably not! That was long before I had any idea of how much good information and beneficial concepts, wisdom, and experiences are locked away in the pages of unopened books. It was before I realized that many other people had been through what I was enduring. They had found the solutions to some of the nagging problems I was facing. And some of them had chosen to share what they had learned.

This idea is behind one of the successful training tools used by Amway. As new people are brought into the business they are vigorously encouraged to read from a carefully selected list of books designed to assist them in their personal growth and relationships. The average Amway "networker" reads at least one such book a month.

How many books have you read during the last twelve months? Of the ones you have read, how many of them have been on marriage, understanding yourself, child-rearing, or spiritual growth—as opposed to sports or how to make money? Christian bookstore owners consistently tell us that women buy 85 percent of the books they sell. Many of the remaining 15 percent are purchased by pastors. As I acknowledged in the Introduction, this probably means *this* book was purchased for you by a woman, probably your wife. After all, when was the last time *you* were in a Christian bookstore . . . and bought a book?

And if your wife bought this book for you, you are, in all probability, a husband whose marriage isn't what it should be, a man whose *life* isn't what you would like it to be. You're probably reluctant to ask for help; you're probably denying you're even part of the problem. But if your wife has given you this book, think about the unspoken message she may have tucked inside.

As you read this book, take off the blinders and see yourself as you really are. Take an objective look at yourself and your marriage. Think about what you can personally do to make your wife thankful to have you as her friend and partner for life. Think about how you can take back your rightful role in establishing your home, your marriage, on a firm foundation.

Think about this—and wake up, men!

4

LET A MAN
EXAMINE HIMSELF

By sharing my own story with you I hope I've convinced you that if your marriage and your life are not all you would like them to be, part of the problem may be with *you*, not just your wife. To help make this possibility clearer for you, I'd like you to take a timeout right now and work through a brief self-examination.

Because it's often easier to see the problems in someone else's life than in our own, we'll practice this examination by looking at another man's marriage. Near the end of chapter 3 I shared a letter written to us by a wife in anguish. At the end of the letter, she plaintively asked, "Do I deserve this? Is there nothing better for me, a Christian, than to live like this for the rest of my life?"

Let's presume that that letter was written to you by a friend's wife and at the end she asked if you would be willing to talk to her husband. How would you reply? What would you say to him? Would you be able to see clearly what he doesn't seem to be able to see himself? Would you be able to give him some helpful and wise counsel based on what Scripture ordains for the home? Would you be able to convince him that if he has an unhappy wife, he *does* have a problem? How do you think your friend would feel if he knew his wife had sent that letter to you?

Take a moment now and jot down how you would answer the questions below. This is the first of several places in this book where you will be asked to write out your answers to specific questions. I know you'll be tempted to read over these questions quickly without actually writing down your responses. But I urge you to take that extra few minutes. You'll be glad you did.

1. Would you be willing to talk to him? _____

2. What would you say to him? _____
   _____

3. What would you describe as the basic problem he's not seeing?
   _____
   _____

4. What helpful suggestions could you make to him?
   a. _____
   b. _____
   c. _____

5. Do you think you could convince him there is a lot at stake and persuade him to examine himself and look at his own role in what is happening in the family? _____
   If your answer is no, why not? _____
   _____

6. How would you convince him to see himself as part of the problem? _____
   _____
   _____

7. How do you think he would feel when he found out his wife had written to you, his good friend? _____
   _____
   _____

If you have taken the time to answer these questions, you probably discovered some ways you could help your friend and give him some good counsel—if he would listen to you. Isn't it amazing how quickly we can all become experts when the problem lies with someone else?

Now let's presume that in desperation *your* wife sent this letter to your best friend. What success would your friend have in coming to you to open your eyes, to make you see what is happening in your home, to make you wake up? Look back over those seven questions and mentally answer them again from this new perspective. Would your friend have the same results with you that you expect to have with him?

Most of us will have little difficulty in sharing our wisdom with our best friend, showing him what he is not seeing himself. We can all be reasonably effective in telling others what to do. But what happens when the situation is reversed and we are the ones being confronted? How will we react when someone we respect and admire comes to us and lays it on the line?

When those I held dear and respected confronted me about my problems on that cruise ship to Alaska, it was hardly the best day of my life. On the other hand it forced me to take a look at myself and what I was doing to Florence and to myself. How would you react if you went through a similar experience?

If you have so far escaped both a confrontation and having a letter written about you, it does not mean one of these catalysts may not be part of your future! Your wife may be as desperate as Florence was. You may be as blind as I was to the real problems that are happening right under your nose. You may be so close to them you can't see them. Spare yourself the agony of a painful confrontation or the humiliation of such a letter. Wake up now and evaluate your own situation. The self-analysis below is a far less traumatic means to understanding the truth and discerning where you are! It will help you identify those hidden stumbling blocks in your life or in your marriage that may lead to serious disruptions in the future if they are not faced and resolved now.

Take the time to read and answer the questions below. We have found that the Lord never wastes information. If they don't apply to you right now, within a week He will probably bring someone across your path who could benefit from them!

Let a Man Examine Himself: A Questionnaire

Answer each question. Leave blank any that do not apply.

Section A

	Yes	No
1. My wife probably does not feel confident that I will listen patiently when she wants to talk to me.	___	___
2. My wife probably feels she generally has to weigh her words carefully to keep me from getting angry or upset.	___	___

	Yes	No

3. I am generally not satisfied with my wife's efforts to please me sexually.   ____ ____

4. We are rarely able to openly discuss our feelings about sex.   ____ ____

5. I generally feel that I cannot share my hurts and frustrations with my wife.   ____ ____

6. My wife complains that I am too critical.   ____ ____

7. My wife probably does not feel she is valuable and important to me.   ____ ____

8. My wife feels I rarely apologize when I have offended her.   ____ ____

Subtotal of yes and no answers in Section A: ____ Yes   ____ No

Section B

	Yes	No

9. I have a tendency to blame other people or circumstances when things go wrong.   ____ ____

10. I admit I am apt to tell a little white lie if it will get me off the hook.   ____ ____

11. I am usually able to talk my way out of most anything.   ____ ____

12. When I am caught at something I shouldn't have done, my first thought is to make an excuse.   ____ ____

Subtotal of yes and no answers in Section B: ____ Yes   ____ No

Section C

	Yes	No

13. Has your wife said her situation has become unbearable?   ____ ____

14. Has your wife ever told you you are verbally or emotionally abusing her?   ____ ____

15. When you look at what your marriage will be ten years from now, does it depress you?   ____ ____

	Yes	No

16. Do you find yourself often looking at or
commenting to your wife about other women?   ____ ____

Subtotal of yes and no answers in Section C: ____ Yes   ____ No

Section D

	Yes	No

17. Do you sometimes wonder why you were ever
born?   ____ ____

18. Did you know as early as you can remember that
you were not wanted or that your parents really
wanted a girl?   ____ ____

19. Did you feel that in marriage you would have
someone you could depend on to love you?   ____ ____

20. Is it very important to you that your wife
frequently tell you, "I love you"?   ____ ____

21. When you communicate a desire for intimacy
to your wife and she doesn't respond, do you
tend to pout, feel hurt, or withdraw emotionally?   ____ ____

22. If your wife wants to go somewhere without you
does that tend to make you feel depressed?   ____ ____

Subtotal of yes and no answers in Section D: ____ Yes   ____ No

Section E

	Yes	No

23. Do you tend to feel sexually frustrated in your
marriage?   ____ ____

24. Are you afraid to ask for a raise even though you
know you deserve one?   ____ ____

25. Would your children say you get angry a lot?   ____ ____

26. Do you find it difficult to forgive people who
have hurt you?   ____ ____

27. Do you feel that your wife is constantly
criticizing you?   ____ ____

	Yes	No

28. Do you have an impulse to "get even" when someone cuts you off on the road? ____ ____

29. Have you gotten violently angry at any time in the past two months? ____ ____

30. Are you and your wife apt to have arguments over finances or purchases? ____ ____

Subtotal of yes and no answers in Section E: ____ Yes ____ No

Section F

	Yes	No

31. Have you ever been emotionally involved with another woman because she understood your feelings? ____ ____

32. Has your wife begged you to go to counseling with her? ____ ____

33. Have you ever suspected (or even known) that your wife was having an affair? ____ ____

34. Does your wife periodically blow up with anger? ____ ____

35. Do you feel that your wife tends to avoid spending time with you? ____ ____

36. Do you feel that your marriage has become less satisfying in the last five years? ____ ____

37. Has your wife complained to you that she is sick and tired of your making her feel stupid? ____ ____

38. Do you tend to hide the family financial status from your wife, especially if it's bad? ____ ____

39. Does your wife complain that you won't help her with the decisions affecting the family or with the disciplining of the children? ____ ____

40. Does your wife think you put her down in front of other people or that you tell her to be quiet so she won't embarrass you? ____ ____

Subtotal of yes and no answers in Section F: ____ Yes ____ No

Total of all yes and no answers: ____ Yes ____ No

Your answers to these questions will help you examine and evaluate your life and your marriage. The more yes answers you gave the greater the urgency there is for you to recognize where you and your wife are in your relationship.

Ten or fewer yes answers would indicate a relatively healthy relationship. You are probably working out most of the issues and questions that are normal in any marriage.

Twenty yes answers would indicate a struggle is going on between the two of you rather than the two of you working as one to build and grow.

Thirty yes answers mean you both need to promptly take stock of where you are before your marriage crashes. You, as the husband and the head of your marriage, need to ask yourself, Where am I failing to understand the needs of this family and see that my loved ones are fulfilled?

Thirty-five or more yes answers show the alarm bell is already ringing. Ignore it at your own peril and risk! *Get help now!*

The six subsections of this self-examination can also help you identify the nature of the problems you are facing. Most of these questions have been adapted from our book, *Get a Life Without the Strife*, which is designed to help you be your own counselor and understand yourself, your reactions, and your relationships in a short time with a minimum of study.

Section A of the questionnaire deals with communication in your marriage, the ability to express your feelings and needs to each other without contention.

Section B addresses the area of emotional maturity. Yes answers here point to the need for growth in this area.

Section C revolves around the need for a loving confrontation to create awareness of the need for change.

Section D will help you identify the presence of childhood rejection issues in your own life that may be making it impossible for you to be fulfilled as a man. *Get a Life Without the Strife* would be an excellent resource for you to start with for help in this area.

Section E helps you see the internal and external stress factors that may be throttling your marriage relationship.

Section F points to the fact that deep roots of hurt or pain may exist within you. Until these roots are identified and weeded out any other efforts to achieve harmony may be simply putting band-aids on deep wounds.

Now that you have completed this self-examination you have three choices: One, you can elect to do nothing and take the risk of whatever comes. Two, you can deny that there are any problems or, if you admit there are problems, deny that there is any hope for resolving them. Or three, you can look at the self-analysis you have just completed and determine that by the grace of God you are not going to be in this same position next year. Resolve that you are going to do something about changing the course of your marriage and your life. You are not going to accept the status quo, you are not going to deny that there is hope for improvement, and you are going to do whatever you have to do to become the man and the husband God wants you to be. Our Lord commends us, "Now that you know these things, how happy you will be if you put it into practice!" (John 13:17 TEV).

In the next chapters you'll learn some of the key factors the Lord has taught me that have brought such satisfying joy into my own marriage after so many years of strife and struggle. Use them to create joy, peace, and fulfillment in your own marriage.

5

OPPOSITES ATTRACT

"Oh, I wish my husband could be here to hear this!"

This is one of the most common reactions Florence and I get when we speak and teach about the four different personalities. Has *your* wife told us this? Has she come home from one of the conferences or retreats we have participated in and said something similar to you? Or after reading one of Florence's books about the personalities, such as *Personality Plus* or *Your Personality Tree*, did she say to you, "Honey, they must have been peeking in our window. This book describes you and me to a T"? Another thing wives tell us they say to their husbands is, "Now I understand why you are the way you are!"

If your wife said something like this to you how would you respond to her? The wives who have shared with us what they've told their husbands have also shared their husbands' responses. Here's a sampling:

- "Oh, that's ridiculous; it's just a theory. I don't believe in any of that stuff."

- "I don't need to hear about it. You can't go around putting people in little boxes or putting labels on them."

- "Are these so-called four personalities in the Bible? If they're not in Scripture, don't bother telling me about them."
- "Honey, I'm really busy. I don't have time to get into this right now."
- "That's fine for you women to get excited about, but I've taken those kinds of tests at work, so I already know all about myself."

Do any of these responses fit the kind of answer you might give? Women so often tell us, "I'd love to share this with my husband. I wish he would listen to me when I get home, but I know he won't. He never does."

Why do we men have this reputation? Is it because we really don't take time to listen to our wives?

Could it also be that we stay disinterested in them so we can avoid conversations that might lead to subjects we don't want to talk about?

Could it be that we really don't want to think about anything that might touch on our emotions and feelings or, even worse, how our wives feel about us?

Could it be that we would rather do anything than get involved in introspection?

I hope in this chapter I can give you a short summary of the things your wife may have learned about the personality types. Florence has such a unique gift of being able to teach the personalities with both depth and humor that she can make the whole learning experience fun. So if your wife has been to one of our seminars or retreats or read one of Florence's personality books, she's probably made a fascinating discovery about your relationship, and she wants to share that knowledge with you. But perhaps you said no. Perhaps you were too busy, too disinterested, too suspicious of this topic. Perhaps if you couldn't or wouldn't discuss it with her, your wife handed you this book and hoped I would tell you what she wanted to say.

And even if this isn't your situation at all, I hope in this chapter I can share some of the enthusiasm I feel for this topic. Studying the four personalities, Sanguine, Choleric, Melancholy, and Phlegmatic, has been one of the most rewarding things Florence and I have ever done. We have been studying, learning, and teaching about these temperament types for more than twenty-five years now, and we never cease to be amazed at how valuable they are. They have helped us understand each other and then to help others do the same. We have literally seen marriages take on a new healthy glow, a new vitality, when these simple truths are understood.

Seeing Each Other in a New Light

The personalities are fun, and they are liberating. Hundreds of spouses have written to us, and hundreds more have told us in person that understanding the different personalities has enabled them to see each other in a whole new light. No longer do they have to try so hard to change their mate into being like them. It is such a simple but life-changing concept. If God created each one of us and gave each one his or her own unique personality, then we shouldn't try to improve on what God has already done perfectly!

Yet that's what I tried to do for Florence for the first fifteen years of our marriage. I didn't realize that God was well-pleased with His creation when He created Florence. I loved her sparkling personality; that's one of the reasons I married her. But there were just a few rough spots I thought could be improved, and I was quick to think I could help her be better. I assumed she would want to be better; I thought she would appreciate my help. What a fool I was! My "help" became so frequent Florence began to wonder, "Why did I ever marry the only person in the world who didn't like me?"

It was Tim LaHaye's book, *Spirit-Controlled Temperament*, that opened our eyes. We learned that we each had a basic, or dominant, personality and a secondary personality as well. Florence proved to be a Sanguine-Choleric, someone who wanted to be in control and have fun while doing it. I found that I fit perfectly as a Choleric-Melancholy, someone who wanted to be in control also, but wanted everything to be done right. For me, fun didn't matter. In my scheme of things there was no place or time for things that were trivia or fun. To me, life was serious and we needed to occupy our time and energy with only those things that kept us heading toward the results.

Once Florence and I identified our personality types, we quickly found out why we were struggling. First of all, since we were both loaded with Choleric characteristics we realized we both wanted to be in charge. This meant we often pulled in opposite directions in a contest of wills instead of working together. This hardly led to harmony between us; instead, it drove us apart. Because I tended to win most of the time, Florence began to feel insignificant and therefore unappreciated.

In the high school where she taught, all her students had loved and respected her—maybe even adored her. What a letdown to enter a marriage that was no fun! Being married to me was not at all what she had expected it would be. What I needed most from Florence was constant affirmation of her love for me. But since I didn't make her feel appreciated, it was difficult for her to be loving. Because she didn't feel I appreciated her, she didn't give me the constant affirmation of love I needed. In response, I criticized and corrected her, trying to make her into the kind of wife I needed. Can you see the vicious circle we were trapped in? Instead of creating the kind of wife I needed, I pushed Florence until she found it increasingly difficult—and eventually almost impossible— to give me the love I so desperately craved.

When we began to understand the four personalities, we got our first glimpse of what we were doing to each other. After becoming Christians, this was the second most important aspect of our lives. It helped us resolve our problems and create the relationship we have today. Now, finally, after more than forty years of marriage, we are not only best friends, we are more in love than ever before. (A third important factor also helped bring us to this point. In chapter 8 I'll share the bombshell discovery that brought about the emotional cleansing I so desperately needed.)

Of course, learning what our personalities were didn't mean we became instantly adapted to a perfect match. But we could at last identify our areas of conflict. For example, not only did we have conflict in our area of similarity (the fact that we both were Cholerics who wanted to be in control), we also had conflict in our area of difference. Florence's Popular Sanguine and my Perfect Melancholy personalities were diametrically opposite. We didn't see *anything* from the same perspective!

She wanted to be spontaneous; I wanted to stick to a schedule. She loved to talk and tell stories and considered silence to be equivalent to "dead air" on the radio; I *liked* a little silence once in a while. She wanted to be with people all the time; I wanted us to be alone. She liked things to be bright and flashy; I thought everything should be toned down and conservative. She liked to be noticed and draw attention; I hated to be in the forefront.

I could not leave the house with dirty dishes in the sink. Florence didn't even notice—and worse, didn't care! I prided myself on always being ready on time. She never even knew what time it was! I always hung up my clothes as soon as I took them off. She left hers wherever they landed! I squeezed my toothpaste tube neatly from the bottom. She paid no attention to the right way to squeeze it—and refused to learn! While my motto for life was always, "If it's worth doing, it's worth doing right" her motto seemed to be, "Then it's not worth doing at all!"

Knowing our personality traits enabled us to see that God had created us this way, so we should not try to change each other and we should not try to change ourselves. In effect, that's what Florence had tried to do in order to please me and to cope with my emotional demands on her. This led her to put on a "mask" and become an unreal and unnatural person.

As a result she ended up not liking herself, and I didn't like her either. She was no longer the person I married. I had forced her to become a phony.

We learned that each personality type has certain definable and predictable strengths and weaknesses (which I'll describe later in this chapter). Yes, even I, the Perfect Melancholy, had weaknesses! They were listed right there on that chart I made when we were inviting friends into our home to share what we had learned. When I put them down on paper it was all too clear.

With this new knowledge we could, for the first time, look objectively and see those things we needed to individually focus on improving—such as the things in ourselves that made us difficult to live with. Seeing those weaknesses enabled us to do what the Scriptures direct us to do: "Let a man examine himself" (1 Cor. 11:28) and "Search *me* O God . . . See if there is any offensive way in *me*, and [if so] lead *me* in the way everlasting" (Ps. 139:23–24 NIV). This was the beginning of the end of the downhill slide and the beginning of our return to the top of the hill.

Recognizing Our Strengths and Weaknesses

One of the laws of physics also holds true in personalities: Opposites attract each other. I was originally attracted to Florence's opposite strengths, and she was attracted to mine. We could see in each other qualities that we admired, which, in general, were ones we didn't possess ourselves. Our strengths fill in each other's weaknesses, making us whole. The Scripture teaches us, "Therefore shall a man leave his father and his mother, and cleave unto his wife: and they shall be one" (Gen. 2:24).

I have an acute sense of time. Florence has little or none. I am strong where she is weak. We tend to fill in each other's gaps. We become one. Our life involves constant travel to speak at retreats, conferences, and seminars. We average about six to eight flights a week. Airplanes don't tend to wait for you just because you got involved in conversation and lost track of time. Because I have, as Florence describes it, a digital clock in my brain (plus a tiny alarm clock in my pocket), we have agreed that I am always responsible for getting us to the airport and to the right gate on time. We have never missed a flight because we arrived too late. (However we have had a few close calls when I forgot to set my alarm! Yes, even we perfectionists occasionally make a mistake.) The very few times when we are not together and Florence has to catch a flight on her own, she says she really feels the added stress this puts on her.

Husbands' and wives' strengths do complement each other. When we men, instead of focusing on or complaining about their weaknesses, learn to appreciate our wives for their abilities, especially in those areas where we are not strong, it makes all the difference in the world. Try this for yourself. You will gradually develop a new and deeper appreciation for your wife, and she, in turn, will be able to respond openly and warmly to you, which is what God intended.

I can almost guarantee this will happen to you *unless* you have already destroyed your ability to recognize her strengths and appreciate her for her abilities. Then it will take some extra time to tear down that wall between you and rebuild your marriage. It may take time for your wife to feel secure enough to trust you once again. And even when you have removed the wall and the emotional trust has been restored, there may still be problems in your wife's ability to respond to you openly and warmly. This may have **absolutely nothing to do with you.** It may be directly the result of things she experienced as a child. How to understand and identify these issues will be discussed later in chapter 9.

Characteristics of the Personality Types

Hundreds of men and women have told us that understanding their personality differences and learning to accept each other was the single most important factor in restoring their marriage and their ability to communicate with each other. In the remainder of this chapter, I'll summarize the characteristics of the different personalities and some of the typical masks that husbands and wives sometimes wear in order to cope.[1] In Appendix A you will find the Personality Profile Test that you and your wife can both take to help you gain understanding about your own personality differences. Also included in Appendix A is a chart showing the strengths and weaknesses of each of the four personalities, as well as a chart showing how the personality strengths can be carried to extremes.

Sanguine

The Popular Sanguine, which is the vivacious, spontaneous half of Florence, is an appealing and enthusiastic storyteller. Sanguines are people-oriented, and they love being the center of attention. Their bouncy and buoyant cheerfulness can be described as charming and even child-like. They are inspiring and expressive, emotional and creative. In telling favorite anecdotes they will never let the facts get in the way of a good story. They don't mean to exaggerate or lie; it's just that the details are not important to them. If they tell the same story five times, it may be different each time, but they never tire of it as long as it gets a good response.

Sanguines make friends easily and they thrive on compliments. If your wife is a Sanguine, tell her each day how great she looks. She'll love it.

With the wonderful Sanguine strengths, though, come some accompanying weaknesses. Sanguines have a tendency to talk so much they often monopolize conversation. When our children were growing up, we had two Sanguines in the house, Florence and our daughter Marita. They tended to dominate all talk at the dinner table. Since there were five of us, I finally had to make a rule that each person could only have 20 percent of the conversation! That was the only way the rest of could ever say a word!

Sanguines tend to be self-centered, always wanting the spotlight on themselves. They are apt to be loud, forgetful, and undisciplined, and one of the greatest problems they cause for others is that they frequently interrupt. One of the reasons they do this is because they aren't listening. They are just waiting for you to pause or take a breath, then they jump right in. They think what they have to say is much more interesting than what someone else is saying.

Choleric

The Powerful Cholerics are born leaders: dynamic people who are always moving, going, and producing. They are strong-willed and decisive, confident and not easily discouraged. If something is out of place they will fix it, change it, correct it, or straighten it out without being asked or told. They are naturally self-motivated and are happiest when they have done something that "couldn't be done." Cholerics prefer to work alone, believing they can get the job done much faster that way. They are usually brimming with self-confidence and invariably they think they are right. Cholerics prefer to be in the control position.

When carried to extremes these wonderfully productive strengths of the Choleric become pronounced weaknesses. Cholerics are apt to be bossy, impatient, and inflexible with people who aren't moving fast enough (in their opinion). They are not impressed with displays of emotion or tears and are not often complimentary. They often will make decisions for you, manipulate you, or dominate you if you are not alert. One of the most difficult things for Cholerics to say is "I'm sorry." They rarely see their own mistakes or their lack of consideration. If it had been done their way in the first place it would have come out right and there would be nothing to apologize for!

These two personalities, Choleric and Sanguine, often occur in combination within one person.

Melancholy

Perfect Melancholies are the thinkers, planners, and organizers—the people who are interested in every detail. They are serious, sensitive, and self-sacrificing. They are schedule-oriented and can always be depended upon to be on time. They love to make charts and graphs. They like to visualize everything on paper before making a decision or solving a problem.

Melancholies are easy to spot just by looking at them. Their hair will be perfect, their clothes will be neat and tailored, their desk or work area will always be neat and orderly. Women Melancholies' handbags will be small and neatly organized, containing only what they need today. They always know where everything is because they always put everything back in its proper place. Melancholies set very high standards for themselves and expect everyone to meet them as well.

When the Melancholies' perfectionist standards are carried to an extreme, they may become easily depressed because others aren't doing things right. Their standards are often too high for others and may even be unrealistic. When others fail to perform as Melancholies expect they may be critical and unforgiving. They sometimes spend so much time planning and organizing, waiting until everything is right, that they never get around to starting the job! They become easily discouraged by others' mistakes and are apt to become withdrawn and remote.

Like the compatible Sanguine-Choleric combination that exists within many people, the Melancholy-Choleric is also a natural and compatible combination. However, in the extreme this person is apt to be the most manipulative and controlling to live with.

Phlegmatic

So far I haven't said much about the fourth personality type, the Peaceful Phlegmatic. In our family we didn't have any! But the gentle, easygoing Phlegmatics make up fully one-fourth of our population. They are usually the most balanced of the four personalities. This may make them more difficult to recognize because they have no very obvious characteristics, no pronounced strengths or weaknesses. They have a low-key personality and fit in easily anywhere and with everyone. They are pleasant to be around because they are relaxed, calm, and patient. They are not apt to speak until spoken to, and they will rarely venture an opinion, especially if it is apt to be controversial. They avoid confrontation at all costs and dislike making decisions. They do not want to be held accountable or responsible when something goes wrong. When Florence would take her Phlegmatic mother to the ice cream shop offering three dozen flavors, which one do you think her Phlegmatic mother would always choose? It was always predictable, unimaginative, noncontroversial vanilla, the safe flavor!

With all these pleasant strengths, it is hard to believe the Phlegmatic has any bothersome weaknesses. If you have a Phlegmatic as a friend you probably can't identify any weaknesses in him or her. However, if you live with this peaceful personality you will quickly find that Phlegmatics do have their share of weaknesses. The two most troublesome are their almost total absence of enthusiasm and their unwillingness to make any kind of decision. Well, yes, they have made one all-time decision; they've decided never to make any decisions! That way they can never be held accountable or blamed. Since they usually marry Cholerics who like to make decisions, it's not really a problem until the Cholerics want them to take a stand on something. But the Phlegmatics either can't or won't. They tend to be watchers rather than doers and therefore may become careless and lazy. They are much more content with things as they have always been and are resistant to change. The Phlegmatic easily pairs with either the Melancholy or with the Sanguine for a personality combination.

This overview of the four personalities is only to give you a basis for understanding the wife you are living with, to help you see that different is not wrong, and that since opposites attract she has many qualities you don't have. I hope this can help you see that together you can make an excellent team when you both function in the home and in your relationship in your strengths, rather than in your weaknesses.

Now let's look at the most common combinations of personalities.

Natural Combinations of Personalities

Most people have a combination of personalities, with one more dominant than the other. Some of these combinations are quite compatible. These are the "natural" combinations:

1. Sanguine-Choleric   2. Choleric-Melancholy

3. Sanguine-Phlegmatic   4. Phlegmatic-Melancholy

When some people take the Personality Profile Test (see Appendix A) they score evenly for three personalities, or sometimes even all four types have fairly even scores. This usually is the result of masking, living in a personality role that is not natural for you, one that is not your God-given birth personality. We'll talk more about masking a little later.

Unnatural Combinations of Personalities

Some combinations of personalities are *not* compatible. These are the two "unnatural" combinations: Sanguine-Melancholy, which is frequently seen, and Choleric-Phlegmatic, which is less common. Both of these combinations contain characteristics that are so diametrically opposed to each other they could not exist together in harmony, as God has ordered, within one person. They are coping mechanisms, masks to help one survive in a difficult or traumatic situation. It's like being an actor on a stage. It takes energy to be someone you are not. Recognizing that you are wearing a mask is the first step to tearing it off and being your real self.

Masking

Now let's take a closer look at some of the most common personalities people try to wear in an attempt to cope with trying situations. Could your wife possibly be wearing one of these masks?

The Sanguine Mask of Popularity and Humor

This mask is frequently put on by those who are not Sanguines in hopes of becoming the center of attention. These people want to be popular, and they use attempted humor to cover up the pain they feel inside. They are often victims of childhood feelings of rejection. By drawing attention to themselves they try to compensate for their feelings of low self-worth and being unloved, unrecognized, or unappreciated.

Sometimes parents pressure their non-Sanguine children to be cute and adorable to show off for their friends. Trying to be funny and bubbly, the child then puts on this Sanguine mask, a mask he or she may wear for a lifetime.

Choleric Mask of Power and Control

This mask can be put on by those who are not Cholerics when they are moved into a position where they have to take control, perhaps because of an absent parent or spouse or when a high degree of dysfunction exists in the family. *Somebody's got to take charge here . . .* they think as they take on this unnatural role. This mask is often accompanied by frequent outbursts of anger resulting from the unnaturally heavy load this person has been forced to carry.

Melancholy Mask of Perfection and Pain

Non-Melancholies may put on this mask when they perceive that perfection is the only standard in their families or when they learn through domination or abuse that this is the only way to cope with and perhaps end the demanding or threatening treatment.

This is one of the most common masks. It is especially common among Sanguine children who quickly learn that their spontaneous, free-spirited personality is unacceptable. It is also commonly worn by Sanguine wives whose controlling, manipulative, Melancholy-Choleric husbands constantly make them feel stupid or sloppy.

The Phlegmatic Mask of Peace and Submission

Non-Phlegmatics may put on this mask when they realize that trying to offer an opinion or take charge is futile. They tell themselves, *Just try to keep your mouth shut, agree with them, and learn not to care.* This mask can be put on during childhood or as an adult. At some time the people wearing this mask have said to themselves, *If I can just stay out of trouble long enough, I can make it through the day.* Suppressed Cholerics who have learned to pull back and not make waves are frequent wearers of this mask.

When you take the Personality Profile Test in Appendix A, if you score in three or four of the columns somewhat equally or if you score yourself to have one of these unnatural combinations, you have most likely put on a personality mask at some point in your life. Remember it takes energy to be an actor, pretending or working at being somebody you are not. Acknowledging that you may have been playing a role and then discovering the reason for it will enable you to remove the mask and be the person God intended you to be.

Looking Behind the Mask

If it's possible that you have forced your wife to conform to what you expected of her and in so doing she has had to put on one of these masks, be courageous and go to her. Tell her you are beginning to see what you have done to her. Tell her you are learning that it is not your responsibility to improve upon what God has created. Tell her, "Honey, it was those very qualities that attracted me to you in the first place!"

Ask her to forgive you and ask her to take off the mask she has been wearing to try to please you. Then . . . ask her to help you see when you are inadvertently, or out of old habits, putting that pressure on her again.

Be prepared for a startling reaction. When I began to say these things to Florence, she was dumbfounded. I had to remind her often that I really did want her help. The road back was not easy or without hurdles, but we have made it—and it is worth the work! You can make it too. These concepts and tools give you the resources you need to understand the problem and help you finish your journey.

Causes of Masking

In our work with thousands of people and our study of the personality types we have identified the following ten causes of masking:

1. A domineering parent. A parent who constantly requires the child to conform to the personality he or she wants the child to have forces the child to wear a mask, usually to become like the parents. Melancholy parents, for example, relentlessly try to make spontaneous Sanguine children into meticulously neat Melancholies like themselves.

If you had such a parent (or grandparent) check here: _____

_____ Check here if you suspect your wife had such a parent (or grandparent).

2. An alcoholic parent. A child who has an alcoholic parent feels pressured to perform or contribute to the household, often assuming parental roles that are not natural for his or her God-given birth personality—or for any child. A child growing up in an alcohol- or drug-based dysfunctional home may soon feel responsible to repair the chaos around him or her. This is especially true when there are younger siblings the child perceives as being neglected.

If this describes your childhood home check here: _____

_____ Check here if you suspect this may describe your wife's childhood home.

3. A legalistic religious household. In this type of family, everyone is expected to be spiritually "advanced," living up to the letter of the law. All family members must conform to what the controlling parent determines is acceptable attitude and behavior. In this setting children are so sanctified and sterilized that no natural personality, no matter what it may have started out to be, has much of a chance of ever growing into healthy maturity.

If this describes your childhood home check here: _____

_____ Check here if you suspect this may describe your wife's childhood home.

4. Strong feelings of rejection in childhood. Children can grow up in homes with well-educated parents, a lavishly decorated bedroom, and plenty of money and still feel rejected or unloved by one or both parents. The issue is not whether these children *know* they are loved but whether they *feel* loved. Often parents are so busy earning money or just struggling to keep ahead of the bills they have little eye-to-eye contact with their children. They perceive that the giving of money or gifts or providing household essentials satisfies the children's need for time and love. Virtually all children who have suffered any form of abuse or were adopted grow up with feelings of rejection, abandonment, or of not having felt loved.

Did you at any time feel unloved as a child? If so, check here: _____

_____ Check here if you think your wife felt this way as a child.

5. A single-parent home. A child reared in a single-parent home, especially a first-born, may often be required to fulfill some of the roles of the absent parent. When these functions are not consistent with the child's natural personality, he or she is apt to put on a mask that will generally be worn in adult life. In a divorce situation when the child is moved back and forth between the parents, the confusion may be even greater if the parents have differing sets of standards and expectations.

If you grew up in a single-parent home check here: _____

_____ Check here if your wife grew up in a single-parent home.

6. Any form of verbal, emotional, or physical abuse. One of the surest ways to warp children's personalities and cause them to put on a mask is to abuse them in any way. Harsh, critical words with implied feelings of worthlessness leave long-term, even permanent scars on children. Many parents who consider themselves to be loving disciplinarians are in fact taking out their own insecurities, frustrations, and anger on their children. They have such a high anger level from their own issues they quickly lash out at the first child who makes a wrong move.

If you grew up with at least one parent (or a custodial adult) who used vulgar or insulting language, who belittled your talents and abilities, or who punished you severely, check here: _____

_____ Check here if your wife did.

7. Childhood sexual interference. Sexual interference is any form of touching the child sexually or having the child touch the adult (or another child) in an inappropriate manner. It is an interference in God's design for the healthy development of the child's mind, body, emotions, *and personality*. Such violation is inevitably a cause of masking, particularly when it is done by a parent or a person playing the parental or authoritative role. The child subconsciously rationalizes, *Maybe if I would just be good enough, he (or she) would leave me alone.* This is especially a cause of adult masking when the knowledge of these childhood experiences has been completely repressed until it is totally unknown to have occurred.

Are you aware of or have you ever suspected sexual victimization in your childhood? If so check here: _____

_____ Check here if you are aware of or suspect sexual victimization in your wife's childhood.

8. A domineering and controlling spouse. This type of mate can have a similar effect as a domineering parent in childhood. For example, a strong Melancholy-Choleric husband may try to change his Sanguine wife into his concept of what a wife should be, namely perfect and productive like he is—neat, tidy, serious, and purposeful. After such remaking, she may perceive herself to be Melancholy-Phlegmatic when in fact she is wearing a mask to cope or survive in the marriage.

Do you think your wife is trying to make you over? Do you feel stifled or domineered? If so check here: _____

_____ Check here if you think your wife would say she feels dominated or controlled by you.

9. Feelings of rejection as an adult. Adults can also suffer feelings of rejection from such things as loss of a job, being passed over for promotion, or losing friends, spouse, or children. Other causes might include being made to feel worthless, feelings of exclusion, or inferences of stupidity. These take on added significance when they are repeatedly reinforced by someone such as a spouse or a boss who is respected, admired, or needed. As a cover-up for how he or she really feels, this adult may put on a mask to help himself or herself feel better about the circumstances.

If, as an adult, someone or something has made you feel useless, worthless, or unwanted, check here: _____

_____ Check here if your wife ever said you make her feel this way.

10. Abuse received as an adult. This may be any type of abuse—verbal, emotional, physical, or sexual—received after the age of eighteen. If you felt hurt or ashamed when it happened, it may be considered as abusive. Instead of finding someone who would spend the rest of her life meeting your needs, complimenting you daily, and loving you unconditionally, you may have experienced abuse from the person you married. Perhaps you have denied it was abuse, rationalizing, "She doesn't realize how her comments hurt me" or "She just has a lot of anger in her; it's not her fault." When you are denying or even lying about this behavior you are putting on a mask of survival to fool yourself as well as others.

If you have frequently felt this way check here: _____

_____ Check here if you have ever abused your wife or physically hit her.

Now go back over these ten causes of masking and count the number of statements you have checked about yourself. If you have had any confusion about your personality, the numbers you have checked on the right side of the page should help you focus on why you sometimes feel the way you do about yourself. The ones that you have checked on the left about your wife should give you a much clearer understanding about who she is, how she feels, and why she may have reacted or failed to respond to you.

For further study, enlightenment, and understanding on personality masking, I would strongly urge you to read Florence's excellent book, _Your Personality Tree_ (Word, 1986). It is her _advanced_ book on the four personalities and will give you a wealth of valuable insight.

If you checked statements 8, 9, or 10 in relation to your wife, I would urge you seek help as quickly as possible from someone you respect and in whom you can confide. One of the best ways to start would be to show these pages to your wife and ask her if she agrees with your assessments. If she does, ask her to give you an honest answer to this question, then _listen without interrupting:_ "Do you feel I am still doing this? Has there been any improvement in the last year?"

If you have asked her for her honest feelings, be prepared for them, even if they aren't what you hoped to hear. Remember she has a right to her feelings. They are not right or wrong, so resist the temptation to tell her "that's not true." Such a response would slam the door shut on your ability to communicate with each other. Listen to her answer. Listen to her feelings. Listen . . . _really listen!_ Your willingness to hear what her heart is saying may be the most important thing you can do to rebuild your relationship.

Almost all personality tests given in industry and business are based on these very same concepts, even though they may use different terminology. Perhaps you've taken one of those tests at work, accepted its results, and put them to use. Now do the same in your marriage; take the initiative in rebuilding your relationship, in learning to understand each other, in finding out why each of you functions the way you do. Don't be ashamed to admit it if you're afraid of what you might find in doing this self-analysis. Don't worry about what your wife will think of you if she really knows you and learns what goes on inside you. Don't be afraid if you are vulnerable to the thought that your wife will not respect you. Don't hold back, leaving things as they are just because change might be uncomfortable for you. Take the lead. Make the change. You'll be amazed at what can happen.

Before we end this overview of the personality types, I'd like to leave you with some basic personality axioms. Think about how each of them could apply to you and your wife:

1. We marry opposite strengths . . . and then go home to live with opposite weaknesses.

2. Just because she is different . . . does not mean she is wrong.

3. Any strength carried to an extreme becomes a weakness.

4. Don't try to change your wife. Even if you succeed you won't like what she becomes!

5. "Accept one another . . . just as Christ also accepted us to the glory of God." (Rom. 15:7 NASB)

6. It is not the personality label that is important but recognizing that each of us has certain definable and different strengths and also weaknesses as well.

Let's show our women we have the courage to examine ourselves, to face our own problems, to cease blaming others, and to be the kind of men our wives can look up to, admire, and respect.

Let's be the heroes our children will want to emulate!

Let's wake up, men!

6

WHY CAN'T A WOMAN . . . BE MORE LIKE A MAN?

God created man in His own image, and He looked at what He had made, "and behold it was very good" (Gen. 1:31). Then God said man should not be alone, so He created woman in His own image. And this creation was also very good! But it was also different. God created woman to complete and to complement man, and His purpose is that man should also complete and complement woman. He created us to be *different*, with different bodies and different functions in life, in the family, and in the home.

If we have different bodies, different functions, unique personalities, and separate strengths and abilities, then it stands to reason that we must also have different *needs*. But how can we meet these needs, including the important emotional needs, unless we know what they are? We men tend to look at our women and expect that what is important to us will be a high priority for them too. We usually don't even begin to comprehend that their emotional needs may be radically different from ours.

We have learned, first from our mothers and then from our wives, that women tend to cry and get emotional more than men. We have learned that they seem to have much greater need to talk about feelings than we do. They seem to need each other more then we need other men. When we come home from work, we want to stay home and relax; they want to go out and do something. Rex Harrison asked the question for all men when he sang, in *My Fair Lady*, "Why can't a woman be more like a man?"

Emotional Needs from Childhood

Florence grew up in Haverhill, Massachusetts, living in three rooms behind her father's convenience store, a rented facility on a commercial street. They had no house, no yard to play in, and only one bedroom for the five of them. The store was their living room. As Florence describes it, this was "hardly elegant living" for this would-be princess! Florence remembers as a child hearing her mother regularly ask her father, "Will there be enough money for us to eat next week?"

In contrast, I was raised in New Rochelle, New York, in a large, comfortable home on a cul-de-sac at the bottom of a hill. It was a safe place, a great place for children to play. Florence called my family home a mansion when she first saw it. The first floor included a large foyer, a living room, library, dining room, kitchen, breakfast room, and maid's room. On the second floor there were four large bedrooms and two ample bathrooms and a wide, open hall that overlooked the foyer downstairs. Above this was a large attic we used for storage. I knew of many other homes that were far bigger and certainly more luxurious than mine, so I never gave a lot of thought to my own home. Although there were some difficult times financially for my parents during the Depression, as a child I was never consciously aware of them. Surely I never dreamed that my lack of appreciation for this home was one day going to be a prickly thorn in my marriage. But it would. Because of our different childhood homes Florence and I would have a big gulf in our understanding of what *home* meant to us in our marriage.

Differing Needs and Sufficiencies

As a child Florence grew up having two new dresses a year and one new pair of shoes—if her parents could afford them. This partially contributed to her self-image of being plain and unattractive. My mother, a careful manager, was thrifty with our family finances, so my younger brother and I often wore our older brother's "hand-me-downs," but we were never without. Clothes and other material possessions were never an issue.

Later in our marriage as Florence and I learned to be vulnerable with each other and discuss our feelings, we realized how significantly our childhood experiences impacted our adult emotions. We could see that what were *sufficiencies* for me became emotional *needs* for her. She had felt the lack of house, money, and clothes as a child, but these things had never been a concern for me. I was never able to understand her *need* to buy more clothes when our money was tight. I couldn't grasp why having all the household bills paid on the day she thought they should be was so important.

When we did have our own share of serious financial problems and had to sell our home to settle some debts I had accumulated in business, I could not relate to the pain and anxiety Florence experienced. She felt I had betrayed her. I wanted at least empathy for the struggles I was going through to try to keep my business afloat, the financial foundation for my family. To me selling our home and moving into the much smaller condominium was simply a necessary change dictated by economic conditions; happiness with our home was not dependent on its size! All I could see was that Florence was materialistic and not supportive of me.

To Florence, the home we sold was her dream house. We had selected the choice lot overlooking the mountains in San Bernardino, designed the house and built it to fit all our desires. Florence decorated it to fit her personality. This home was important to her; it fulfilled much of what was important in life to her at that time. Leaving it was a loss I didn't share. But it triggered the old childhood fears of insecurity and feelings of deprivation she had never verbalized. To me it was just a house, and Florence's inability to emotionally let go and get going was materialistic—definitely not spiritual!

Those were difficult times for both of us. We didn't understand each other's basic emotional needs that had originated in childhood. We didn't see that Florence's needs were my sufficiencies. The things that were important to her in childhood, the things that had become her emotional needs, were things I never had to think about or struggle with as a child.

But as we began to examine ourselves and our relationship, we looked at the things that were good and healthy in Florence's childhood. She always felt loved and valued. She always felt encouraged, especially by her father, who was her number-one fan. Despite the lack of material things in her childhood, she remembers her home as a fun place where she, her two brothers, and her father, all Sanguines, always had a good time. Her Phlegmatic "vanilla, please" mother sat on the sidelines and tried to give some serious balance to all the family fun. Florence's sufficiencies were love, approval, and family fun.

Then we thought about what I felt I lacked in my childhood, my emotional needs. I didn't lack house, clothes, or money. But as a child I had never felt loved. I *knew* I was loved, but I never *felt* loved. I felt I had to earn love by doing everything right or by doing it better. Later we learned the term for this: I was a victim of *rejection*. In recent years we have learned that there was more. I'll share that with you in a later chapter.

As we continued to think about my childhood, it was clear that since I didn't feel loved and felt I had to earn love, I didn't feel approval either. I never felt any recognition or approval for what I did accomplish. And perhaps since there were five children in my family I, as the middle child, never felt I got any support for the things I wanted to do, for my dreams or aspirations. I had to figure things out on my own without any guidance. In defense of my family, I can now freely admit that I was a difficult child and did not take direction, discipline, or counsel very well. My brothers and sister would probably say "that's more than an understatement!" But none of us, back then, had any idea why.

Florence's sufficiencies were love, approval, and family fun.

My sufficiencies were house, clothes, and money.

My needs were almost identical to what she had in abundance: love, approval, and support.

On the other hand, things that were adequate in my childhood—house, clothes, and money—were emotional needs for Florence.

To further complicate our inability to grasp why the other spouse was hurting was the fact that my needs were internal and intangible while Florence's needs were external and material.

When we finally understood our emotional needs we were able to see why selling Florence's dream house was so traumatic for her and was just another chapter of life to me. We were also able to understand why I felt so hurt and unloved by Florence's attitude. I wanted her to be happy *with me* no matter where we lived. I didn't want her love for me to be conditional on where we lived, but that's the way it felt. I even remember asking her to tell me she loved me enough to live with me in a tent if that was all we could afford. I needed to hear that kind of affirmation. But she was not able to even mouth the words! This triggered within me all the unresolved conflict resulting from my childhood sense of rejection.

Unlocking these unrecognized truths and then understanding how they were affecting our relationship was the first step in finding the freedom from this insidious bondage. Today we can talk about it and laugh, where once just mentioning it might unleash a flood of exposed emotion. Now we know that hiding emotions in no way solves the problem or fools the person we're trying to hide them from. Our wives don't know why we're acting the way we are, but they certainly know something is wrong. As a result they handle whatever is going on inside us by avoiding us or dancing around the problem. Hardly the way to build a healthy marriage relationship!

Reaching Out to Our Wives

To be able to fulfill each other's emotional needs you're going to have to find out what they are. If we men are going to be the heads of our families, we are going to have to take the initiative in identifying these needs. The head of the family should be the first one who's willing to say, "Tell me how you are feeling. What did I say that made you feel that way? Let me be your friend. I want you to be able to trust your emotions to me. Even though what you say may make me feel hurt, I promise you I will not get mad. I will not interrupt you. I will not tell you you're wrong." If we did risk saying those things and then if we did get mad or interrupt or say "that's not true" or "you're wrong" then we must be man enough to quickly confess our failure or weakness and ask forgiveness of our wife. Hearing you say, "Honey, I'm sorry. Can you forgive me?" may be the next important step in rebuilding the feeling in your wife that you are a man she can trust and respect.

It is not unmanly to listen to your wife express her emotions—or to express your own. We men have to get it out of our heads that emotions are for sissies. That lie was programmed into us when we were little by some well-meaning soul who told us, "Big boys don't cry!" Even Jesus, the strongest, most courageous man who ever lived, was not ashamed to show emotion. He was the "man of sorrows" (Isa. 53:3). He "wept" (John 11:35). He "had to be made like His brethren in all things . . . since He Himself was tempted" (Heb. 2:17–18 NASB).

Assessing Your Unfulfilled Childhood Needs

Now it is time for you to think about your own childhood needs and sufficiencies to see if they may still be holding a grip on you. Take the time to think about what was missing in your childhood and to what extent you are aware of it. If you are not aware of any unfulfilled childhood needs, ask your wife to help you think through these things. She may be thrilled to find out you are thinking introspectively for a change!

My Childhood Needs	My Sufficiencies
1. _____	1. _____
2. _____	2. _____
3. _____	3. _____

My Wife's Childhood Needs	Her Sufficiencies
1. _____	1. _____
2. _____	2. _____
3. _____	3. _____

Your answers on the lines above will probably not be the same as Florence's and mine were, but you may be surprised to find that your unfulfilled childhood emotional needs are very similar to what your wife had plenty of as a child. And those things that were abundant in your childhood may have been totally absent from your wife's growing-up years. Seeing these differences can help you understand your emotional responses to various things you have faced in your life together. Talking, sharing, and communicating your feelings about these issues are major steps toward breaking through the emotional blackmail the devil may be using to trap you. We men need to start exchanging the lies we have accepted for the truth that will set us free.

Adult Emotional Needs

Just as spouses' childhood needs may differ, so can the adult needs of husbands and wives be significantly different. On numerous occasions when we have been speaking to a group of women, we have asked them to list the ten things they, as women, want most out of life or out of their marriage. Listed below are ten of the most frequently mentioned criteria wives have given us. After looking at this list—and at the brief summary that follows—write in the far-right column what *you* want most out of life and out of your marriage. List those things that are important to you personally, not those you think might be important to men in general. Just list them as they come to you. They don't need to be in any particular order. Ignore the A and B columns for now. We'll use those later.

Women's Emotional Needs:	A	B	My Emotional Needs:
1. Security	___	___	1. _____
2. Affection	___	___	2. _____
3. Understanding	___	___	3. _____
4. Appreciation	___	___	4. _____
5. Communication	___	___	5. _____

Women's Emotional Needs:			My Emotional Needs:
	A	B	
6. Respect	___	___	6. _____
7. Unconditional love	___	___	7. _____
8. Acceptance	___	___	8. _____
9. Support	___	___	9. _____
10. Companionship	___	___	10. _____
Totals	___	___	

Other needs the wives gave less frequently included feeling needed, feeling desirable, receiving consideration, intimacy, encouragement, attention, patience, and time with their husbands. Many others were also listed, but the ten above were clearly the most important. Before we move on, put a bookmark here. You'll be coming back to this page to evaluate your own adult needs after a quick summary of what the words on this list mean for most wives.

1. Security. To receive the fulfillment she deserves in exchange for being selfless to her man, a wife must feel secure in him. This includes financial security. It also includes the secure knowledge that she is the focus of her husband's needs, that he is not looking at, thinking about, or involving himself with another woman. Our wives' greatest single need is security. If they are not secure in our love for them, our provision for them, and our protection of them, they will struggle in fulfilling their God-ordained roles in the marriage. We must be worthy of their love. When a wife is simply unable to fulfill her natural God-given desire to be a helpmate, there are other valid causes that go beyond her willingness to do so. Those valid reasons will be addressed later.

2. Affection. When our wives speak of affection, they are not referring to sex. They are referring to the soft, gentle, tender look they see in our eyes that tells them we love them, that we accept them just the way they are. It's the look that says to them "I'm glad I'm married to you." It's the way we touch them. It's the way we hug them. It's that connection that says "You are special and important to me." It's the one that doesn't have a hidden agenda (heading to the bedroom).

3. Understanding. One of the biggest complaints wives share with us is that their husbands have all kinds of demands and expectations of them, but never have any interest in the stumbling blocks or hurdles they have to overcome just to get through a typical day. We'll get much further with our wives if we let them know we care how their day went, if we show an interest in the things that are important to them. When we don't, we force them to find a best friend elsewhere. When this happens we are apt to get jealous because they are not spending their time with us and not confiding in us. Becoming an understanding husband takes only a little willingness and a little determination.

4. Appreciation. I used to have a very bad habit. When I would come home from work I would notice everything that was out of place, everything that was undone, or all the requests I had made in the morning that had not been completed. Try as she did (and I must confess Florence did the best she could) I never seemed satisfied. Instead of hearing my complaints that dinner was not quite ready on time, she desperately wanted to hear me appreciate the things she had done during the day. If she had washed the kitchen floor, she wanted me to get wildly excited about how great the floor looked and to ignore the fact that the breakfast dishes were still sitting in the sink. And after praising her for what she did, it would have been much better if I had just washed the breakfast dishes without any comment about how noble I was to do for her what she hadn't managed to do herself. Now I have learned to do whatever I can for her. For example we've come to share the morning breakfast duties: I make breakfast and she cleans up. Sometimes, however, when she is under stress or short on time, I'll tell her, "You go and get ready; I'll clean up the kitchen."

"But you made breakfast," she says. "It's my job to do the dishes."

"No, Honey," I say. "I have more time than you do, and I'm happy to do it."

Does this make me appear weak? On the contrary, Florence respects me because she knows now, finally, that I always try to think of her first. She knows my objective is always to try to protect her, not only physically, but emotionally. I try to anticipate everything that might happen, and I have learned to both appreciate her and everything she has accomplished. She has learned to appreciate me as well. It's meant some work, but it's been worth it.

5. Communication. The biggest stumbling block to building better and healthier marriage relationships is spouses' inability to listen to each other, to hear what the other is really feeling, not simply the words he or she is mouthing.

Florence has said, "Many of us communicate with our spouses as if we were actors in a boring play that will never make it to Broadway. We have learned what lines we can deliver effectively, and to keep the creaking show alive we respond consistently to the same cues. There's not much spontaneity or mystery because we've learned if we stray too far from the routine we'll get in trouble."

That certainly was the way we communicated for many years. Once Florence said, "When I heard Fred tell another man, 'Florence and I have no problem communicating' I was stunned! We talked about nothing with emotional meaning. I realized I had played my role so well I deserved an Oscar."

Many men don't realize how much better their marriages would be if they allowed their wives the freedom to respond honestly. Breaking out of this mold caused Florence and me more conflict than any we'd had before. But after a while our communication became *real*, and talking to each other became fun. Men, let your wives be real; give them permission to say what they think without judgment, even if it doesn't agree with your opinions.

6. Respect. For many years I tended to put Florence down in front of other people. Most of the time I didn't even realize I was doing it. I thought I was simply correcting her—so her story would be accurate, for example. Somehow I thought I had a right to do that. I had insisted on high standards of perfection for myself and expected them of Florence as well.

But what I actually communicated to Florence and to those around us was a lack of respect for my wife. Those who had deeper perception must have seen that I subconsciously did this because I had such a low self-image of myself that I tried to make myself feel superior by emotionally knocking Florence down. I have now completely changed course and I focus on building her up and edifying her according to Ephesians 4:29, which happens to be the theme of her inspiring book, *Silver Boxes: The Gift of Encouragement*. Has this improved our relationship and her perception of my respect for her? About 1,000 percent!

7. Unconditional love. Read the "love chapter," 1 Corinthians 13. What's described in those verses is unconditional love, the kind of love the Bible says a man must have for his wife. This is the kind of love our wives desire from us and have a right to expect. Does this describe how your wife perceives your love for her?

8. Acceptance. Your wife needs to feel accepted for who she is, how God created her, and what she can bring to your marriage relationship. Instead, many wives feel their husbands are trying to change them into being something else. Some husbands make their wives feel unworthy or stupid; they don't listen to their wives' opinion. They act like they think God ordained them to make all the decisions. They make their wives feel as though they were only born to serve them, and they don't treat their wives as beautiful, fragile flowers—that is, with respect. Understanding your personality differences can help you see that your wife is worthy, perhaps more worthy than you in many areas. Our wives' strengths fill our weaknesses. If the God who created her accepts her, should you not do the same?

9. Emotional support. For the most part, God created man to be rational and woman to be emotional. He created man to be physically stronger and often more emotionally stable. Our wives understand this. They have no desire to be men; they don't seek our roles. But they do want us to be MEN for them. They want to respect our strength instead of being afraid of us. They want us to use our emotional strength to deal with our anger when it arises so they can trust us. Our wives want to be able to lean on us emotionally. Then they will know they can depend on us to help them see and do what they can't do for themselves. Today Florence says she cannot even think of life without me. That simply indicates how important I have become to her as her emotional support system. How have we made this 180 degree turn? I do everything I can to encourage her and I try to do everything for her that is difficult for her or that she doesn't like to do. You can change the course of your marital ship, too, if you're willing to try.

10. Companionship. My wife wants a friend for life. When she feels hurt or discouraged, she needs me to be the one she can come to. When she thinks about doing something to have a good time, she thinks first of doing it with me. She never could in the past—just the contrary, in fact. When she wanted to have a good time, she learned to do everything she could to make sure I was preoccupied in some other way. Only without me could she have fun. Isn't that pitiful? Major changes were needed before we could enjoy the lifetime of friendship we expected when we married. Most of those changes had to occur in me. Today, neither of us can imagine life without the other. We have become lifetime companions. You can too.

Now that you have an idea what the needs listed on pages 62–63 mean, you're ready to evaluate how well you have done as a husband in meeting your wife's emotional needs. Go back to those pages and score yourself in column A according to this simple scoring scale:

Always = 4   Seldom = 1

Usually = 3   Never = 0

Sometimes = 2

Give yourself a 4, for example, if you feel you are doing an excellent or very good job in providing security for your wife. Bear in mind that women generally tend to think of security as *emotional* security, which includes financial security. It would be hard for a woman to feel emotionally secure if she didn't also feel financially secure. Men tend to think of it strictly in terms of financial security. After you have rated yourself on each of the ten needs, total your score in the space provided.

Discussing Your Answers

Would your wife agree with your answers? Show the list to her and ask if she agrees with the top ten needs the other women have designated. She might switch one or two to more closely describe what is important to her. Chances are she will enthusiastically agree with most of those on the list. Before you show your wife this list, however, go over it one more time. This time use the same rating system, but score yourself in column B according to *how well you think your wife would say you are doing* in meeting her emotional needs. Once again, add up the numbers and get a second total. Do they agree? Are they similar? Are you still willing to show this list and your two scores to your wife to get her reactions?

The first reaction you may expect from her is surprise and delight that you are even reading this book—any book, for that matter, that deals with family issues. The second reaction you may receive is thrilling gratitude that you are focusing on things that are important to her. This will be even more likely if she senses you are sincerely trying to understand what her needs are so you can do a better job of meeting them.

If, on the other hand, her reaction is cynical and full of disbelief, don't give up. Don't throw the book across the room in anger. She could simply be responding from the deep well of pain inside her. There is still hope for both of you. There is still One—there will always be One—who can cleanse and heal all the wounds in either of you. You must be patient. You must be persistent. You didn't get where you are in your marriage overnight, and you won't get where you want to be in a short time either. It takes time and effort—and lots of prayer from both of you. But it's worth it! If God could bring healing and restoration to our marriage, He can do it for yours too.

Do you feel yourself hesitating to share this with your wife? Why not take the time to do it right now? Tell her you have "something in this book I'm reading that I'd like to have your opinion on." (That's always a good way to start. Wives, like most people, are usually flattered when we ask for their opinion.) Show her the list on pages 62–63 and ask her if she agrees that these are important needs for most women—and for her. Tell her you're asking "because I'm trying to understand your needs better." (Before you show her the women's list, cover the list of your own emotional needs with a piece of paper so she can't see what's there.) Then comes the big risk: Ask her if she agrees with your two rating columns. Especially ask her about column B, in which you indicated how you think she would rate you. Be prepared! She may not agree with your self-evaluation.

Your wife will immediately sense that for once you are really interested in and concerned about how she feels, particularly if you have avoided these kinds of discussions in the past. This exercise and conversation could open the doors on some of the most meaningful communication the two of you have had in years. On the other hand, it could even be painful. Don't let that possibility stop you from talking together. This kind of healthy, nonconfrontational meeting will richly reward both of you. But it takes courage. Do you have what it takes?

As part of your discussion of these emotional needs, ask your wife which two traits you are doing the best to provide for her. Then ask her which two she feels are the most lacking. Next ask if these are the two that are most important to her for you to work on. If so, circle those two on the list. Then tell her you will commit to her and to the Lord right now to make a special daily effort to improve in these two areas. Tell her you will ask the Lord daily in prayer to help you and give you the discernment to see when you stumble. But remember, if you make such a commitment your wife will be watching to see if you will carry it out. She may have learned through past experiences that some of your commitments are only one-day deep. It would be a good idea to ask her each night to help you evaluate how well you have done on these two issues. Keep a record for thirty days. This can be a most effective part of rebuilding your relationship.

In his outstanding daily devotional book, *My Utmost for His Highest*, Oswald Chambers wrote, "God does not give us overcoming life: He gives us life as we overcome. The strain is the strength. If there is no strain, there is no strength." This is a book we strongly urge you to read each day as a part of your daily devotional time or your communion with the Lord.

You *are* setting aside time each day, a half-hour at least, to be alone with the Father, aren't you?

There are no quick cures, no magical pills, no scriptural band-aids you can put over marital wounds that will bring instant healing to emotional wounds. It takes time and patience, falling down and getting up again, effort and perseverance, forgiveness and letting go, caring and wanting. It takes starting fresh tomorrow. But the results will be worth your effort!

P.S. A note from **me** to **you:** I have learned that many people when they read a book such as this—and this is especially true of men—skip over the exercise portions, sometimes thinking they'll come back to do them later. But they rarely do. Because I am sharing with you the things that changed my life and my marriage, and what the Scripture teaches us men to practice, I have learned what works and what God honors. Therefore I urge you again not to skip over these pages, but to carefully complete everything that is suggested. I think you will be glad you did.

7

OPEN MY EYES, LORD

At a recent retreat for pastors and wives I met a young pastor whose spiritual maturity and commitment to the Lord deeply impressed me. Randy's sincerity and his willingness to honestly look at himself were unusually refreshing. Later he shared with me some of the feelings he had written out as he spent personal time alone with the Lord beside a wide river that flowed just below the conference center.

As I look out over that wide expanse of moving water, slowly carrying its burden of silt and debris, I am struck by my own spiritual burden. It is an invisible weight that holds me back, keeps me from moving ahead with my dream of being a pastor.

The burden is the hurt I have inflicted on my wife. I am an outgoing, people-oriented person, and she is not. Often I've been bothered by her shy manner, her preference for being alone, her discomfort at being around others who seem louder, more expressive, *happier*. I have been hard on her, trying to make her change and fit my mold for her. And the memory of my actions haunts me and robs me of the spiritual joy I so earnestly long for.

I have been wrong. First Peter 3:7 warns that husbands must respect their wives or their prayers will be hindered. This warning has come true in my life. My disrespectful treatment of my wife has caused her to be like a bud that has not been able to blossom. I confess that I need Your forgiveness, Lord, and I need my wife's forgiveness too. I need to be kinder, more patient and more respectful—allowing the Holy Spirit to fashion her as He wills.

What a confession for a young man to make! I so appreciate that one sentence at the end: "I need to . . . [allow] the Holy Spirit to fashion her as He wills." We could all learn from what the Lord placed on Randy's heart. There is hope for this marriage. This husband is honest and sincere; his eyes have been opened and he has seen what his controlling nature has done to his wife. Now he can begin to make the changes in himself that will allow his wife to be the woman God created her to be. Because he is a man of prayer and is not ashamed to talk openly with his Father in heaven, he will come to the Lord for guidance and understanding. This the Lord will surely give him. Oh, the anguish and heartache I would have spared Florence if I had heard such words years ago—and if I then had done something about them.

Too often we men have eyes that do not see and ears that do not hear. And when we do not hear the truth we cannot act on it. Sometimes we are *blind* to the circumstances we have thrust upon our families. Other times we see what is happening, but we *deny* that we could have had anything to do with it. We are so quick to blame others, and we know so well how to exonerate ourselves. If we can shift the blame, we can also shift the responsibility. Then we can fool ourselves into believing and saying, "It's not my problem!"

At that same retreat where I met Randy I also happened to sit at lunch one day with a delightful woman named Ruth. As we chatted she asked me if Florence was my wife. When I proudly said yes she was thrilled. She had read several of Florence's books so we had an immediate bond. She said she was in full-time ministry herself and her husband, who hadn't come with her to the retreat, had pastored for many years but wasn't pastoring anymore. She was ministering alone to new ethnic Christians and regretted that she didn't have his support or participation.

She asked me how I felt about being the husband of a well-known wife. "Was it threatening for you?" she asked. "How did you handle that?" she wanted to know. She didn't think most men could cope. I shared some of my own testimony of the tremendous healing God has done in me and in my marriage. I told her of the three books I had already written and of my ministry to Christians who had been victimized as children.

Then I mentioned to her that Florence and I were currently writing companion books, *Wake Up, Women!* and *Wake Up, Men!* Ruth was immediately interested, especially in my book. Her husband surely did need to wake up, she said, adding, "If it were not for God's unconditional love and the affirmation of many Christian friends, I would feel hopelessly useless. My husband doesn't seem to have any interest in anything anymore. He pays no attention to me and just lets me do whatever I want to do. He doesn't want to pray with me. He'll never tell me how he feels about anything. I know he's miserable inside but he won't let me get close to him even though I long to help him. We've been married thirty-two years, but we're as far apart as any two people could be. I wish I had what you and Florence have." Later Ruth wrote to me,

> I so appreciated your willingness to be open and discuss your process of healing. The transformation God has worked in you is wondrous. I just wish my husband would be willing to reach out to get what you have gotten. I hunger for communication with him. I yearn for him to affirm me as his lover, his woman, his playmate, his friend, and his prayer partner. If only he would be vulnerable enough to share his heart-felt feelings with me before God. But instead he shields himself from all but the most minor interaction.

What a tragedy. Not only is this ex-pastor wasting his own life, he is squelching the spirit of his wife as well. What does she have to look forward to in the coming years with her husband? Where will this marriage be in ten years? If it weren't for the effective ministry she is having with foreign-born Christians, she would feel "hopelessly useless."

What a contrast Ruth's husband is to Randy. Ruth's husband is still blind, but Randy can now see. Randy recognizes he has fallen short, and he's working to become the man God wants him to be. He is asking God to help him be the husband his wife needs so her bud can blossom. But what hope is there for Ruth? Will her husband ever change?

I gave Ruth a copy of our book, *Get a Life Without the Strife*, and told her to pray that the impersonal and objective pages of the book might reach her husband—if he were willing to read it. Sometimes a book is less threatening to us men than a wife's "preaching" at us or telling us what we ought to do.

Are You Genuine or a Phony?

A few years ago Florence met with some of the women on the committee planning a CLASS seminar that Florence would be teaching in their church the following spring. They were concerned about another committee member who was not at the meeting. She had strange, erratic behavior, major mood swings, and often showed a great rage toward her husband; she had even threatened suicide. Florence had already met this woman and noticed her problems; she had no doubt that the woman needed help.

Florence asked if they had talked with the lady's husband. They replied almost in unison: "He is a very prominent professor at the Christian university. We'd be afraid to approach him."

Since Florence was from out of town and therefore "safe" she said, "Well, perhaps I could get him alone for a few minutes when we all get together for dinner tonight."

When Florence met with the husband he agreed with the women's concern for his wife. She was in serious trouble and did need some kind of professional help, he said. He listened politely as Florence offered some suggestions and answered that he was very appreciative that the ladies cared. Then he said, "I thank you for your interest in my wife. I recognize she has some definite problems. But what they don't seem to understand is, I have a very prominent position at this university. If people thought my wife had mental problems, it could ruin my reputation. We'll just have to deal with this the best we can on our own. I can't risk my reputation."

Is this husband blind, or is he in denial? Apparently he does acknowledge his wife's problems; he sees that she is hurting. But he seems totally unwilling to put her needs ahead of his own misplaced sense of importance.

How do you feel about him? Is he someone you could respect and look up to as a man? Is he someone you could trust your deepest feelings to? Many of us would regard him as a phony who is not worthy of the reputation he has carefully cultivated for himself. If he were your professor, your Sunday school class teacher, would you want to listen to his pontifical pronouncements?

We men need to begin thinking of how we appear not so much to others as to our wives and children. Are we worthy of the respect we expect from them? Do they see us as genuine or phony? Do they hear us preaching one thing and then doing something completely different? Do we teach our children not to lie and then instruct them to tell callers, "Dad's not home" when we're standing right there beside them? Do we smile politely when we walk into church on Sunday morning, giving the impression that we are "blessed in the Lord" when in fact our family members weren't even speaking to one another in the car on the way there? Aren't we all guilty at one time or another of these examples of double-mindedness? Isn't it time we men wake up and be the honest and upright leaders of our homes and families we want our wives and children to think we are? The seeds we sow today will be reaped in the too-soon future. Let's look objectively at our gardens and root out the things that are growing toward destruction. If the job is too big for us alone, we should not be afraid to cry out for help before it is too late and the flowers are completely choked out by the weeds. To paraphrase the Scripture, "what profiteth a man if he wins the world but loses his family?"

Eyes That Do Not See

A pastor who had been to one of our Promise of Healing Workshops went back to his church in Australia so cleansed and renewed he knew he had to share what God had done for him. At the next service he told his congregation that at the workshop the Lord had clearly revealed to him that his father had sexually violated him when he was just a little boy.

He told his flock that through the prayers for healing following this retrieval of his totally repressed memories he had found an unbelievable peace and freedom. He told them he also found a richer and deeper intimacy with the Lord because he had broken out of the bondage he hadn't even realized he was in. He said he knew the anger problem he had struggled with all his life was already being cleansed away. And he encouraged his church family to dig at the roots of whatever might be keeping them from being all that God created them to be.

After he finished speaking, one of the elders stood up in the service and loudly took issue with what he had said. He proclaimed angrily that as Christians everything is covered under the blood and we are not to go back to look at past issues. In front of everyone else the elder told the pastor he should not stir up trouble like this. Later another outspoken elder came up to him to say he agreed with the first elder. These kinds of things should never be discussed in church, he said. It could cause all kinds of problems.

When the pastor told us this story we asked him, "What are they hiding? It reminds us of the quote from Shakespeare's *Hamlet*: '[Thou] doth protest too much, me thinks.' These elders seem to be protesting too much. Why weren't they rejoicing with you in what God had done for you?"

"Well, I can tell you why," he answered. "Both of those men's daughters have come to me in the past and confided to me that their fathers interfered with them when they were little. Neither of the men know that I know or that their daughters even are aware of it today. But I can tell you, both of those young women have been through a lot of struggle in their lives, and now I have a better understanding why."

Were these men in denial? Were they hiding something? Had they been blinded? The answer to all three questions is obviously yes. They are denying that those compulsive acts of twenty-five or thirty years ago have any significance today. They are hiding their pasts for fear those long-ago events might be exposed, revealing who they really are. They have been blinded to think that "leaving well enough alone" is the best answer to any question that might be emotionally threatening.

These men need to be like Randy. They need to come out from behind the wall of protectionism they have built, see what the real problems are, and be willing and courageous enough to face them. Then they need to find the answers that will enable them to change their course.

The same is true for all of us. We men need to open our spiritual eyes to see the true state of our homes, our families, and our marriages. Our Lord said, "If your eye is bad, your whole body will be full of darkness. If therefore the light that is in you is darkness, how great is the darkness!" (Matt. 6:23 NASB).

We need to surrender our egos to the Lord and ask Him to guide us into all truth. As Christian men we need to acknowledge where we have fallen short and come to Him and cry out, "Lord, help me!" and know that He will. But this isn't always easy to do. It even took Jesus' disciples awhile to understand the power of this wonderful promise. The eighth chapter of Mark shows this when it describes what happened when, after the Lord had fed the multitude, He and the disciples sailed in a boat to the other side of the Sea of Galilee.

> And they had forgotten to take bread: and did not have more than one loaf in the boat with them. . . . And Jesus, aware of this, said to them, "Why do you discuss the fact that you have no bread? Do you not yet see or understand? Do you have a hardened heart? Having eyes, do you not see? And having ears, do you not hear? And do you not remember, when I broke the five loaves for the five thousand, how many large baskets full of broken pieces you picked up? . . . And when I broke the seven for the four thousand, how many large baskets full of broken pieces did you pick up?" And they said to Him, "Seven." And He was saying to them, "Do you not yet understand?" (vv. 14, 17–21 NASB)

Facing the Storms of Life

When Fred Parker, district supervisor for the Four Square Church in the Great Lakes District, spoke at the dedication of the church in Red Wing, Minnesota, he gave a powerful and relevant message based on Jesus' words in the seventh chapter of Matthew:

> "Therefore everyone who hears these words of Mine, and acts upon them, may be compared to a wise man, who built his house upon the rock. And the rain descended, and the floods came, and the winds blew, and burst against that house; and yet it did not fall; for it had been founded upon the rock. And everyone who hears these words of Mine, and does not act upon them, will be like a foolish man, who built his house upon the sand. And the rain descended, and the floods came, and the winds blew, and burst against that house; and it fell, and great was its fall." (Matt. 7:24–27 NASB)

As Fred Parker spoke, he said there are two constants and one variable in this passage and in our lives as well. The two constants are the house and the storm. Each of us in our lifetime in some way builds a home. Where we build it, how we build it, and what materials we use will make a big difference, because the second constant is the storm. Each of us will face storms during our lives.

As surely as there is a tomorrow, those rains will descend, the floods will come, and the winds will blow. How will your house stand against the storms of life? How will your family handle the crisis if you lose your job? Is there a safety net built into your family finances to tide you over until you find new work, or are you living to the max on your credit cards?

How would you react if your wife confessed to you that she had had an affair but that it was over and she was asking you to forgive her? Could you forgive her? Would you blame her and make her grovel at your feet? Or could you ask her, "Honey, where have I failed you that you were even interested in looking at another man?"

What would happen if your teenage daughter came home and told you she was pregnant? Would you quickly send her out of town to get an abortion so no one in church would know? Are your relationships with that daughter such that she could even risk telling you? Or would she get an abortion by herself so you would never know?

What would you do if your wife came and told you that she just found out that your younger brother molested your five-year-old son?

These are some of the storms that families we know have had to face. You no doubt have already faced your own share of trials, and most likely the Lord will allow each of us to face additional storms in the future.

Consider those two constants in the passage from Matthew: the house and the storms. And think about the one variable: whether we build our house on the rock or on the sand. If we have founded our house on the rock, the Scripture says it will stand. Or maybe we can just *pretend* we built it on a rock. Maybe we can even make our neighbors believe we have built it on a firm foundation. Then when the rains come and the foundation shakes, we can put our blinders on and try to believe if we don't look at the storm it will go away and if we don't talk about it, maybe there's really no problem after all. Or we can deny that it is even raining or that the winds are blowing. We can just get into bed, turn up the radio, pull the covers over our heads, and say, "As far as I can tell, there's no storm. I can't hear anything and I can't see anything."

Fred Parker pointed out one more thing about this house we are building: Whether we have built the house on a rock or on sand, whatever the foundation, *we are going to have to live in the house we have built.*

With that reminder, let's open our eyes and take a good look at the house we are building. Let's ask the Lord to make us willing to face the truth about our shortcomings. Let's ask Him to show us the things we are missing, the things we have overlooked. Let's ask Him to show us what other people see in us. And finally, let's be willing to see any sin that is still festering in us, anything we have not been willing to fully face and deal with.

Search me, O God, and know my heart: try me, and know
my thoughts: And see if there be any wicked [or offensive] way
in me, and lead me in the way everlasting. (Ps. 139:23–24)

If we need a little immediate help and direct answers, we could always begin by asking those who live with us. They will have no problem helping us—if they feel they can trust us not to jump all over them if they take the risk and open their mouths.

8

THE WRECKER OF MARRIAGES

I have already shared with you that for most of my adult life a lot of anger boiled within me. I had learned from the counselor in 1987 that much of it came from that old suitcase of emotional hurts, the one labeled REJECTION that I had carried into my marriage. I also accepted the fact that I had done such a masterful job of suppressing the anger I didn't even know it was there. It was triggered by Florence's inability to meet my emotional needs, most of which were unhealthy, unrealistic, and self-centered cravings and yearnings.

But as I look back on the years of my adult life, the decisions I made, the chances I took in business, and the way other people perceived me, I now can clearly see that there was much more amiss than anger and an unhealthy need to feel loved. I now am able to recognize other, more ominous symptoms that were binding every aspect of my life. I can see them now, and I've learned their dark, ominous source. Yet only seven years ago I would not even have recognized their existence, identified them as symptoms, or given them any significance.

Symptoms of a Secret

I had a critical spirit during these years. I was so critical, in fact, that Florence felt nothing she ever did was right in my eyes. No matter how hard she worked, I could always show her how to do it better or I could point out the one thing she overlooked. I noticed only the negative.

I had such a strong "need to be right" I would even go to excessive lengths to prove that I was. If something was amiss in our home, I would not only point it out, I would insist on finding out who was responsible. For example, "Who left the door open so the flies could come in?" Florence helped me see that I was not content until I had placed blame—and she got in the habit of accepting that blame even when it wasn't true, just so we could go on! We learned that this habit pattern also had childhood roots.

As I analyzed my career, I saw that I had a repeated tendency to make high-risk choices, especially when business or profit was poor and therefore our family income was low. When I was in the auto-repair business in San Bernardino, to help build volume I began doing repairs for customers on credit. I felt I was offering a valued service to people who needed their cars for work but could only afford monthly repair payments. I convinced myself this was noble. I did everything I could to protect these high credit risks. Before long I was selling used cars on credit to the same kinds of people. On paper it looked very good in both volume and profit. But where are those cars today? Gone. They disappeared. And where are the unpaid invoices representing thousands upon thousands of uncollectible dollars? They fill two file boxes in a warehouse. Today I can see how foolish I was back then. But back then I was blind! Today I can see the tremendous pressure this poor judgment placed upon my wife and children as well.

I believe I made these numerous high-risk and poorly thought-out decisions because I needed to be a winner. I needed to prove I was worth something. Deep within my soul I must have had serious questions about my own sense of self-worth. But I hid those feelings so well only an expert would have seen it. It was covered not by an inferiority complex, but by a *superiority complex*—perhaps the sense that I was invincible, that I could make no serious mistakes. And when I did make mistakes I was able to rationalize to my wife, to myself, or anyone else who might have been involved that they were not my fault. I had become a master in placing the blame on someone else so I never had to face the responsibility. The sad result of this process was that I never learned from these mistakes. I kept repeating the pattern over and over.

Connected to my feelings of superiority, or perhaps self-righteousness, was an inability to receive counsel. I am sure, in fact *Florence has told me*, that on numerous occasions people had tried to get my attention, to warn me, to alert me to what was going on or to what I was doing. But I was blind to reality. I couldn't even see what they were talking about, or I simply did not hear them. I also had what I now describe as selective vision. I only saw what I wanted to see.

Another factor was tied in with those described above. For lack of a better term I will call it the "right to be questioned." This trait was particularly pronounced in our home, where the emotional dynamics most frequently unraveled. Florence has shown me, and I am now able to admit, that I strongly reacted whenever I felt threatened by her questioning my wisdom, my judgment, or my decisions. She learned the kinds of topics that were too risky to bring up, and she avoided those questions out of fear. Had I been able to listen, I would have spared myself—and my family—much grief. We have learned from the many hours we have both spent with wives and with couples that this is a common problem in many homes.

There was one more symptom that was, as I look back, so glaring I should have seen it myself. But of course I didn't. It is a symptom that is so common among men we think it is normal, that everybody does it. It is the obsessive interest in the female body. Let me clarify: It is perfectly natural for a man to admire and appreciate the female form. God created that healthy trait in us. However, when the focus becomes *obsessive* this is clearly an aberration from God's creative design and an indication of some dysfunction.

I would prefer not to admit it, but there is no gain in pretending. If I were not honest and vulnerable, I would have nothing to share with you beyond textbook knowledge. I am now aware that I owned these dysfunctional symptoms in varying degrees for fifty-eight of the first sixty years of my life. Some of them did not appear until adult years. But I now know they commenced when I was two years old.

Do some of these symptoms apply to you as well? On the list that follows, check each symptom that has ever applied to you. Don't rush through the list. Think for a moment. Has anyone ever ascribed one of these traits to you or said you never . . . or you always did one of these symptoms? In addition to my own symptoms described above, a few more have been added and space has been left for any others you might think of.

Men's Symptoms of Adult Dysfunction

____ 1. Feelings of rejection

____ 2. Controlling anger

____ 3. Critical spirit

___ 4. Need to be right

___ 5. Place blame

___ 6. High-risk choices

___ 7. Low self-worth

___ 8. Superiority complex

___ 9. Inability to receive counsel

___ 10. Blind to reality

___ 11. Right to be questioned

___ 12. Sexual obsessions

___ 13. Unexplained fears

___ 14. Inferiority complex

___ 15. Chronic depression

___ 16. Reluctant to trust

___ 17. Judgmental spirit

___ 18. Feeling hopeless

___ 19. _____

___ 20. _____

___ **Total**

The number of symptoms you have checked will give you some idea of the characteristics your wife and family may already have seen in you. It may help you to understand, as I finally did, that any problems in your marriage are not all to be laid at your wife's feet. We men need to accept responsibility for those problems that are ours.

Now that I have described my own dysfunctional symptoms, let me share with you how I learned the root cause of most of them.

September 9, 1989

Florence and I were speaking at a conference in a church in Sydney, Australia. The conference was entitled, "Freeing Your Mind from Memories That Bind," the name of the book we had co-authored. We were sharing the importance of understanding adult symptoms of childhood rejection and sexual victimization as a first step toward restoration.

It was late in the afternoon. I held two photographs in my hand as I encouraged the audience to study their own childhood photos, especially the eyes, to see when a change might have taken place. I held up a picture of a sparkling one-year-old girl already expressing the features of a Sanguine-Choleric. It was little Florence. I handed the picture to a man named Lawrence sitting directly in front of the platform. Lawrence looked at the picture, smiled, and handed it to his wife. Florence, sitting behind me on the platform, was watching.

Next I held up the second picture. It was a picture of me when I was a child: nicely dressed, hair just right, obviously taken in a studio. On the back of the picture my mother had written "Fred Jr., age 2 years and 4 months." I told the group there was a sadness in my eyes in this picture that I have never understood but I presumed there was a reason for it. I handed my picture to Lawrence as I continued speaking. Florence watched as Lawrence looked at the picture, blanched, and immediately passed it on to his wife. He could not look at it.

Half an hour later when the conference ended Lawrence rushed up to Florence to say, "I know Fred was molested before that picture was taken!"

Florence was incredulous. How could he make such a statement? This was Sydney, Australia, half a world away from New York where I was born twenty years before Lawrence. How could he possibly make such a statement?

Quietly but earnestly he said, "I am a child molester. I have molested over a hundred little boys and girls in my life. I have been in prison four times. When I looked at Fred's eyes in that picture, I knew he was molested."

What a bombshell he dropped on me that day! Yet the more I thought about it the more I knew he was right. I already knew the symptoms. I had already been ministering to the sexually victimized for several years, yet I had no conscious knowledge of it ever happening to me. I never dreamed of such a possibility. But when I accepted the possibility the Lord even showed me who my molester was: a housekeeper who had lived with us for twenty years. She had fled Germany in 1931 and my mother had hired her virtually right off the boat.

Three days later I spent two hours with Lawrence and his wife to minister to them at the Sydney Airport, just before we took off for home. He told me of his horrific childhood of sexual interference and the terribly disrupted life he has led since. Two years ago I met the couple again at a Promise of Healing Workshop in Melbourne and was able to hear of the progress he was making in his own healing journey.

Although the Lord had let me know who my victimizer was, I still didn't know what she had done. I felt I needed to know, if for nothing but to have credibility when I spoke on the subject. I was already well along in my own healing.

I began praying for the Lord to show me through memory retrieval what the housekeeper had actually done to me. At first nothing came but a few momentary flashbacks, until one night about a year and half later. Florence and I were once again flying home across the Pacific from another ministry trip Down Under. I awakened during the night and started to pray again, "Lord, show me what she did to me." Instead of answering my prayer as I asked, He showed me more.

A man.

Now I knew I had two violators to deal with. As quickly as the first time the name came to me. It was my elementary-school principal. Once again, despite my asking, there were no details.

Sometimes we need help in uncovering these repressed traumatic memories. I called Star Lysandra Cole, a prayer director in our ministry. I had prayed with her some time before to help her uncover the beginnings of her years of victimization. Now I was the one who needed help. We made an appointment to pray over the phone. The whole scene became very clear as I saw everything the housekeeper had done to me.

But what about the principal? We made another appointment to pray two months later. When we did, I found myself standing in his office. I saw everything that happened. I was eight years old. Both of these experiences (and I believe both happened more than once) had been totally repressed in my memory bank. But they were there all the time. These childhood violations were clearly affecting who I was and how I acted, but I had absolutely no conscious knowledge or memory of them.

Cleansed by the Savior's Healing Power

Was it valuable to uncover these memories? Was it necessary?

Remember my main objective in knowing the truth was to be credible, not to bring about my healing. That was already well under way, but the healing I was experiencing was for the rejection issues! The memory retrieval greatly enhanced and expedited my recovery, which has happened through my daily coming to the Lord in prayer. Jesus offers all of us this same invitation: "Come to me, all you who are weary and burdened, and I will give you rest" (Matt. 11:28 NIV).

Today all those dysfunctional symptoms I described earlier are gone. They have been cleansed away by the incomprehensible healing power of the Savior.

In chapter 5, I said there were three important factors in bringing Florence and me to the happy, fulfilling marriage we have today. I said the single most important factor was our becoming Christians. The second was our understanding of the four personality types and how they have led us to understand each other better—and share what we've learned with thousands of others around the world. And this was the third—my becoming free of the memories that had bound me to those hidden feelings of hurt, anger, critical spirit, and the need to prove myself.

Now Florence and I know the joy, the love, and the friendship that God intended husbands and wives to experience. Where I was formerly frustrated and felt I had no option but to spend the rest of my life in what felt like a loveless marriage, I now have the most loving, caring, and tender wife any man could ever dream of. What has made the difference? The process began when I was finally forced to take a look at myself and stop blaming Florence. When I was willing to do that, God allowed me to see all the things that were holding me back. He showed me far more than I could ever have anticipated.

The road hasn't always been smooth. There were many hurdles to surmount. But it was worth it! I would say we have made it to the top— except we keep going higher and higher. Our lives together keep getting better and better!

At conferences where we speak, it is not unusual for someone to come to me and say, "I saw you a few years ago. There's something different in your eyes now. They seem so soft and gentle. What has happened to you?"

I love to answer that question. I love to tell them what the Lord has done for me!

He is still doing His good work in me, as promised in Philippians 1:6: "He who began a good work in you will carry it on to completion until the day of Christ Jesus" (NIV). Today the whole focus of my life is to encourage and show men and women who are hurting that there is hope and help, and they *can* have healing from these painful emotional hurts that are rooted in our childhoods. In the next chapter we'll talk about one of the most common adult manifestations of this emotional pain, the inability to enjoy sexual intimacy.

The first step to overcoming these emotional obstacles is understanding their source. To gain insight into these issues, you may benefit from reading other books about recovery from childhood victimization. The following brief list of books was compiled by our associate Star Lysandra Cole, who has found these titles to be the most helpful in her own recovery. She is a good one to ask. She has read more than 150 books on this subject in the past four years.

**Star Lysandra Cole's Recommended Book List for Couples
Facing the Possibility of Childhood Sexual Victimization**

1. *Get a Life Without the Strife*, Fred and Florence Littauer (Thomas Nelson, 1993).

2. *Freeing Your Mind from Memories That Bind*, Fred and Florence Littauer (Thomas Nelson, 1988).

3. *The Promise of Healing*, Fred Littauer (Thomas Nelson, 1990).

4. *Outgrowing the Pain Together*, Eliana Gil (Dell, 1992).

5. *Repressed Memories*, Renée Fredrickson (Simon & Schuster, 1992).

6. *Overcoming Hurts and Anger*, Dwight Carlson (Harvest House, 1981).

7. *Freedom of Forgiveness*, David Augsburger (Moody, 1988).

9

"My Wife Has Little Desire to Be Intimate"

"My wife and I love each other, but she is physically aloof from me. She has little desire to be intimate."

Seeking hope and help, many Christian husbands have come to us with statements like this one from a recent letter. What advice would you give them? How does a healthy husband handle his wife's complete disinterest in physical intimacy? What does he do if he truly loves his wife, but she reacts negatively anytime he comes near her? Does he find someone else who can temporarily satisfy his natural desires? Should he divorce his wife and leave his children to marry this other woman?

Before we begin to consider the options for a Christian husband in this situation, we need to ask a few more questions.

If God created woman to be a helpmate for her husband, why does an otherwise loving and appreciative wife shun intimacy with her husband who, in her heart, she truly desires to please? Is there any hope she will ever change? Is there anything that can be done for her? Is this a condition that can be treated with drugs? Is there any known cause for this lack of desire?

Most husbands who are struggling with this dilemma think they are the only ones experiencing such a scenario. They probably feel this way because men rarely discuss these kinds of issues with each other. (Can you imagine one man saying to a friend, "Tom, my wife and I haven't had sex in almost two months. She doesn't even want to come near me. I don't know what's going on. You got any ideas?") And they rarely seek out the professional counsel that might help them. So they have no frame of reference for comparing their situations.

The reality is that lack of marital intimacy is an all-too-common problem facing countless Christian husbands, and a large percentage of them, approximately two out of three, have no idea what to do about it or why it happens. Most of their wives don't understand it either, so they can't be of much help to their husbands. They grope through years and years of dissatisfying marriage without any hope that there ever can be a change.

Without hope, without knowledge, without understanding, what is the almost automatic conclusion these husbands must eventually draw? That there is something wrong with *them!* They begin to question their own manhood, their virility. *What's wrong with me?* they worry. *Why can't I fulfill my wife? Is it some technique I'm missing? What am I doing wrong?*

If husbands verbalized these hurtful questions their wives would probably answer, "No, Honey, it isn't you. You're fine. You're doing everything right. I just don't know what it is. I don't know what's wrong with me. I freeze up when you come near me. I don't want to and I don't plan to; it just happens. I do everything I can to be the wife I know I should be. Then something happens. I can't be that person."

These may be the very words your wife has said to you if she is unable to respond to you sexually. If she does have an idea why she is not able to respond, she may have told you. Listen to her carefully. Men frequently do not want to accept what their wives are trying to tell them.

For the many men who find themselves in this situation, disappointment turns to dismay, dismay turns to feelings of disapproval, disapproval becomes frustration, and eventually the frustration may turn into full-blown anger. Some men reach this stage quickly. And how does the wife react to her husband's anger? Does it draw her warmly and lovingly to him? Hardly! It only further suppresses her already-stifled emotions, and she becomes even more distant.

The spouses experiencing this painful predicament soon find themselves in a downward spiral. Their whole marriage relationship is affected by irritability, feelings of rejection, inability to communicate, emotional separation, and finally the complete loss of any desire to please each other. This last phase can also appear to be selfishness or self-centeredness. Under these conditions no relationship can grow, much less survive. Scriptural principles for marital harmony are forgotten as the focus of the marriage turns almost exclusively to the negative, to problems, and to self.

In this chapter I'll give you an overview of what we believe, based on our judgment, our study, and our experience in ministering individually to more than two thousand men, women, and couples, is the single most significant factor in causing the adult dysfunctions that lead to a lack of marital intimacy. We'll also identify two other causes of this problem that may be less common but can be equally effective in wrecking a marriage.

Divorce is never the best solution for resolving these issues, even though it often appears to be the only way out. But in divorce both parties automatically become "losers" who become part of a "singles marketplace" consisting, with rare exception, of other losers who have left their own troubled marriages in an attempt to start over. The new entries into the singles scene carry with them the same, old, unresolved issues they've been dragging around most of their lives, but now they also bring along some new adult feelings of hurt and rejection left over from their failed marriages.

No, divorce is not the solution.

But what is?

The answer is *not* that they must simply tough it out. The answer is *not* that they, as Christians, must accept this pain as their cross to bear. And surely the answer cannot be that they have no hope, for that would belie the essence of the gospel message.

The answer to the question lies in the fact that *there is a reason* for this kind of marital dysfunction. There is a root cause, and husbands and wives need to find that cause, accept it for what it is, and be careful not to deny its significance. We Christians, of all people, have the power within us to overcome any obstacles and experience complete restoration. That is our hope! That is our promise!

The Devastating Aftermath of Childhood Victimization

In our eight years of studying and ministering to more than two thousand people about this issue we have found that the single most prevalent cause of adult dysfunction leading to marital stress, including lack of marital intimacy, is *childhood sexual victimization*, It is the taproot from which almost all branches of adult dysfunction spring up.

How do I know? There is no question in my mind that my own symptoms of dysfunction, described in the previous chapter, resulted from acts that were perpetrated against me as a little child. My life was not ruined, but only by God's grace, for I surely came close to making a complete mess of it. And I never knew why until that afternoon in Sydney, Australia. Then it all made sense.

If you think this couldn't possibly have happened to you or anyone you know, consider the statistics generally accepted by informed authorities and researchers. They say approximately 25 percent of all women experienced some form of sexual victimization in their childhood. That figure alone is staggering. This would mean that every fourth husband reading these words is married to a woman who suffered this ordeal as a child! In a survey cosponsored by the Center for Women Policy Studies and reported in the June 1993 issue of *Mirabella* magazine, "more than 27.3 percent" of the seven-thousand-plus respondents reported that they "have been sexually abused."

One out of four, 25 percent!

Now maybe you're wondering, *Am I one of those one-out-of-four husbands?*

It is important to remember that in this survey and any other one like it the response is based only on those who are *aware* of the victimization. There is no reference to those whose memories or knowledge has been completely repressed, as mine was. A comprehensive survey was completed in early 1989 with more than twenty-five hundred respondents, about two thousand women and five hundred men. This survey sought to determine, first, the percentage who had known victimization and second, the percentage who had the same kinds of clear symptoms of victimization but no conscious memory. The results were consistent with the findings reported in *Mirabella*: 23.4 percent of the adult women and 11.1 percent of the men acknowledged known childhood sexual abuse.

The next finding of this survey was even more shocking. An additional 51.5 percent of the women reported having some of the same clear symptoms of violation as the 23.4 percent who were aware of it. These two figures total 74.9 percent of the women! The figures for the men were equally astounding. An additional 54.6 percent reported the same kinds of clear symptoms as the 11.1 percent who had knowledge of abuse, for a total of 65.7 percent of the responding men.

These surveys were conducted in ten different Christian conferences among Christian men and women.[1] Even allowing for a 5 percent margin of error, these figures would indicate childhood violations of 75 percent of women and 60 percent of men!

Is it any wonder that our churches are filled with hurting people who are emotionally struggling to get through each day? Many are fighting battles of spiritual unworthiness, undiagnosed physical pain, and—is it any wonder?—lack of marital intimacy.

Why are these figures and statistics important to you? The first reason is that based on these percentages alone there is a very strong chance that your wife may have been sexually violated as a child. Even if you were to ask her and she said no, that would be no certainty. We have already seen that 50 percent of the women in the survey also said no—because they had no knowledge of childhood interference. It lends credence to what Roseanne Barr Arnold is reported to have said: "There are only two answers to the question 'Were you sexually abused as a child?' The first answer is 'Yes I was,' and the second is 'I don't know yet.'"

The second reason why all this should be important to you is because you need to be compassionately interested in the reasons behind problems with physical intimacy in your marriage, if that is your situation. And don't you also have a personal vested interest in how your wife feels about sex?

The third reason is that if, in fact, your wife was violated, there are very valid reasons for her adult feelings or lack of feelings. Your blaming her for her disinterest or inability will never solve the problem; it will only compound the guilt, the shame, or the unworthiness she may already feel. What she will need from you is huge measures of tenderness and patience. Unfortunately, too many wives report that instead of being patient and tender their husbands are impatient, critical, and thoughtless when dealing with these hurts.

One wife described the attitude that is typical of many husbands: "He doesn't believe in any of this sexual abuse stuff; he insists that looking into our pasts is nothing but a witch hunt. He says we should all be responsible for ourselves." Here are some other typical responses wives have told us their husbands have given after the wives confided they were molested as children:

- That's no big deal. My mother was too. You should be over it by now.

- I don't want to hear any more about it. I just want you back the way you used to be.

- I really don't care about the past. I have needs too.

- Your problem is you haven't forgiven him. You need to pray more about it. Then you can be the right kind of wife.

- Don't blame me if I find someone else who is willing when you're not.

Are any of these responses similar to what you might say (or have already said) to your wife? If there is any chance your wife is among that

25 percent who know they were victimized or that 50 percent who have repressed victimization, it is essential for her, and for your benefit as well, that you become an integral part of her restoration team *today*. She needs your help, understanding, and tenderness. Unless you have studied widely on this subject you probably have no idea how devastating childhood violations are to a woman. Remember: God created man and He also created woman, and He created them to be very different. Generally, women handle these things in a very different emotional manner than men. Your wife needs you to empathize with her feelings.

In this chapter we will focus on the possibility that your wife was victimized as a child because, as you can see in the previously cited statistics, this situation is somewhat more common for women than men. However, keep in mind that what we're describing here could also apply to you, the husband. After reading the last chapter you surely know that I speak from experience!

Gaining Understanding

As a man and a husband you need to know that once a little girl has been inappropriately touched by or made to inappropriately touch any adult man she is very apt to feel dirty and ashamed of her body. Does your wife undress in the closet, in the bathroom, or in the dark? Perhaps now you can understand why. One husband told me he had not seen his wife's body in twenty-eight years of marriage.

As a man and a husband you need to know that many little girls, even three, four, and five years of age, have been orally and/or vaginally penetrated by adult males to satisfy their compulsive cravings. Oral violation is the most common form of victimization of little girls and little boys. During one six-month period I prayed with sixty-two women and a few men for retrieval of their childhood memories of suspected violation. Fifty-eight of them, 94 percent, had been orally abused.

Can you imagine how an adult wife would feel about a similar act if, as a little girl, she had been forcefully and perhaps repeatedly subjected to this? Whether or not she "owns" the memories will make virtually no difference to how she feels about the experience as an adult. The painful emotions are locked away until they are released, cleansed, and healed. Does this give you any insight to your wife's reactions?

There is another way we may be able to help you get in touch with your own feelings about victimization and therefore better understand what your wife may have been through. Imagine that it happened not to your wife, but to your daughter.

Do you have a little girl about four or five years old? Or if you have a daughter who is older now, can you think back to when she was that sweet, tender age? At this stage all a child really knows is to trust and obey: Trust the adults who take care of you, feed you, and clothe you, and obey what they tell you to do. Think of her at that age, and think what your own reactions would be if your wife came sobbing to you, saying *your daughter* just came home crying, "Mommy, Mr. _____ across the street made me put his thing in my mouth!"

Would you believe her? Little girls virtually never make these things up, especially when they volunteer it on their own. Far more frequently they never say anything to anybody! Too often their molester threatens to harm them or a loved one if they ever tell. Or they may instinctively feel so ashamed they *can't* tell. Even worse, they may try to tell but nobody believes them or they are scolded for saying such a bad thing.

One woman, who has only recently become aware of her past violations, remembered that as a six-year-old girl she had tried to tell her mother what Grandpa was regularly doing to her. But her mother, perhaps not grasping what the child was trying to say, told her, "We have to do whatever Grandpa wants because we have no other place to live, and we can't have him throw us out of here." The little girl was trapped. Not only did she have to continue doing what Grandpa wanted without complaint, but she carried the double burden of believing if she didn't she would be responsible for the whole family's having no place to live. What a heavy load for a little six-year-old to carry!

Does it make you feel sick to imagine your own daughter being abused? Do you want to scream when you hear of a six-year-old molested by her grandfather? Do you feel like you want to choke someone? Do you feel like you want to put your fist through the wall? . . . Well, good. Maybe now you can begin to understand some of the pain your wife has endured alone if she was forced into these things as a child.

I am always appreciative of a husband who accompanies his wife when she comes for memory-retrieval prayer. It tells me he cares and is supportive. He will also hear firsthand as his wife receives the repressed memories in answer to her specific prayers. On several such occasions I have seen husbands' anger flare up as they "witness" their wives' violation, knowing there is absolutely nothing they can do about it. There is no way they can protect their wives at this point, as any husband would want to do, because it is something that happened many years ago, long before they even knew each other!

A husband whose wife was victimized as a child becomes the "secondary victim" of her childhood abuse. Because God intends a husband and wife to become *one*, those things she endured necessarily affect the husband as well. There is no way this can be avoided or denied. Instead we men need to be strong enough to be able to say to our wives:

"Honey, I can't even begin to fathom how anyone could ever have done that to you, but I am beginning to see how it has caused you so much pain. And I want you to know that to the very best of my ability, and with the strength and patience God gives me, I will support you and stand by you. I will do all I can to help you work through these issues to find the healing Jesus promises is possible. I know I will stumble, for I can now see that I am a victim, too, of what was done to you. I have my own feelings to work through. But together we can make it."

Living an Abundant Life

Why go through the potentially painful process of uncovering repressed memories? Why not leave well enough alone? By all means, if "well enough" is well enough, then leave it alone! But if things aren't going well between you, why settle for a small piece of life when God wants you to have the whole pie? He said, "I am come that they might have life, and that they have it more abundantly" (John 10:10). If your life isn't abundant then it surely behooves you to find out why. Jesus also said, "You shall know the truth, and the truth shall make you free" (John 8:32 NASB). Retrieval of traumatic suppressed memories is not only scriptural, it is a major step forward in the healing journey. If, as I did, your wife carried an old, invisible suitcase full of hurts into your marriage, she will experience a wonderful new freedom after she unpacks that old luggage and examines the contents. It's not easy to do; nor is it a painless process. But it is freeing and life-changing.

How Can My Wife Know?

The first step is to determine if there is buried trash that needs to be dug out—if there is, in fact, repressed victimization that needs to be identified. This can be readily done by asking your wife to complete the simple and effective survey that follows. This tool has been used successfully in helping thousands learn the truth about themselves, and it has proved to be more than 99 percent accurate.

Before asking your wife to complete the survey, you will want to give prayerful thought to how you are going to approach her. You need to carefully think through her expected responses and feelings and plan your words accordingly. Will she be interested in taking such a survey, or would this whole subject be very threatening to her? Does she tend to get nervous or anxious when such subjects are discussed? If she does, she may refuse to complete the survey when you ask her to. It's not that she doesn't want to please you or do what you ask. She may already have suspected this and be genuinely afraid of what she might find out. Yes, the Bible does say, "You shall know the truth, and the truth shall set you free." But she may not be ready for that. The most important thing you can do is to be sensitive to her needs and feelings. Timing is so important. You may need to pray and ask the Lord to show you the right time to present this to her. Surely you already know enough about your wife's changeable disposition to know that what might be fine one day might be impossible another!

If she refuses to take the survey, or if she says she'll do it "some other time" but never gets around to it, what then? Can you insist, cajole, or demand that she take it simply because *you* want to know her answers? The answer to that question is simply and absolutely NO for two very important reasons.

The first one is that once again we men understand painfully little about women's feelings. To insist or demand might seem to her like a *revictimization*. If a male did violate her as a child, she could perceive your insisting on your right to know about it as a repetition of someone exercising that unknown control over her. By insisting, you could conceivably destroy forever, if not put a major stumbling block in the path of, her ever being willing and able to face these perilous buried issues (if they are there). Once again I urge you: *Be sensitive to her needs*. If she refuses or avoids it, you may simply have to wait until a more appropriate time. Let the Spirit guide you.

The second reason why you must not insist is that you really don't have any right to do so. You don't have any authority to demand this of her, and *even if you did*, would you want to exercise it over such an emotionally delicate question?

"Wait," you may want to argue, "did I understand you to say I don't have the right to insist? Am I not the head of my household?"

Yes, you did understand me correctly, and yes, you are the head of your household. But these are different issues we'll talk about later, in chapter 13, when we discuss what it means for the husband to be the head of the wife.

Right now the issues are (1) Trying to understand the root cause of most problems of marital intimacy, and (2) Trying to determine if any of the symptoms apply to you and your wife. The first step toward these objectives is getting your wife's cooperation and arousing her interest in looking into her past. Achieving that is up to you to tenderly and thoughtfully accomplish.

Survey of Emotions and Experiences
For Women

Check each line that applies or *ever has applied* to you. Note that the blank for each statement falls under one of four column headings, which are explained in the "Scoring the Survey" section on page 98. Leave blank any statements that do not apply or you are not sure of.

	Clear	Strong	Possible	Group
1. Abusive spouse			_____	
2. Afraid of big or black dogs				_____
3. Alcoholic parent			_____	
4. Anorexia/bulimia or other eating disorders			_____	
5. Being chased in dreams	_____			
6. Brother or sister molested as a child			_____	
7. Candles in dreams				_____
8. Childhood "bad houses or bad rooms"	_____			
9. Childhood depression			_____	
10. Date rape	_____			
11. Dislike roses or their smell				_____
12. Don't like full moon				_____
13. Downcast looks as a child			_____	
14. Dreams of snakes		_____		
15. Early-childhood anger		_____		
16. Early-childhood masturbation (before age ten)		_____		
17. Emotionally abused as a child			_____	
18. Emotions suppressed in childhood				_____

	Clear	Strong	Possible	Group
19. Fear of being alone		___		
20. Fear of knives				___
21. Fear of losing weight		___		
22. Fear of rape	___			
23. Feel unworthy of God's love	___			
24. Feeling dirty	___			
25. Fits of rage	___			
26. Guilt feelings			___	
27. Hate Halloween				___
28. Hate men	___			
29. Hear chanting or laughing in dreams				___
30. Hide real feelings			___	
31. Lack of trust		___		
32. Low self-worth		___		
33. Marital sexual disinterest			___	
34. Memory gaps in childhood	___			
35. Migraine headaches		___		
36. Panic attacks	___			
37. People wearing hoods or robes in dreams				___
38. PMS (called PMT in some countries)		___		
39. Poor teenage relationships with boys				___
40. Recurring bad dreams		___		
41. Rejection feelings			___	
42. Same-sex attraction	___			
43. Scared by bells, chimes, or gongs				___
44. Self-hatred	___			

	Clear	Strong	Possible	Group
45. Sexually abused or molested as a child	____			
46. Sexual compulsions	____			
47. Sometimes hear voices				____
48. Spiders in dreams	____			
49. Strange feelings about "the cross"				____
50. Suicidal feelings			____	
51. Teenage promiscuity			____	
52. TMJ (a jaw problem)	____			
53. Temptation to touch children sexually	____			
54. Uncomfortable with nudity in marriage	____			
55. Uncontrollable anger		____		
56. Uncontrollable crying	____			
57. Undiagnosed pains and aches		____		
58. Unexplained fear of darkness				____
Your totals:	____	____	____	____
Possible:	21	14	11	12

Grand total (add all four column totals): ____

Note: This Survey of Emotions and Experiences for Women and the following scoring analysis are adapted from *Get a Life Without the Strife* by Fred and Florence Littauer (Thomas Nelson, 1993). All rights reserved. Used by permission. This form may be reproduced.

Scoring the Survey

Add up her responses in each of the four columns and enter the score on the "Your totals" line (the numbers under each of the Totals lines indicate the possible number for that column). Then add up her four column totals to get her grand total of responses.

If the Survey of Emotions and Experiences has been answered accurately and honestly you and your wife will now be able to identify the root cause if you are facing problems of marital intimacy. Bear in mind that there may be three different root causes. We are focusing here on the first of the three. (The other two, irresponsible husbands and abusive husbands, will be discussed later in this chapter.)

The first thing to realize in looking at the survey scores is that every statement on the list is a possible symptom of childhood sexual victimization or interference. There is one exception, number 45 (number 42 on the men's survey, which begins on page 113): "Sexually abused or molested as a child." It is not a symptom. It is a fact. If there is no mark on that survey line, this means "no" or "does not apply." As far as your wife is *aware* there has been no abuse or molestation. But if that line is marked your wife is indicating she is aware of some childhood abuse. Even when the abuse is acknowledged, if, in sharing with you what happened it doesn't sound to you like anything significant, BE CAUTIOUS! Listen to what your wife is telling you. Do not make light of it! She needs your love and support, but that's not all. Even a seemingly minor molestation at, for example, the age of thirteen, can have deep and disruptive effects. But there is another even more important reason. There may be much more at an earlier age that is completely repressed and causing far greater devastation than either of you is aware or can imagine.

What the Survey Columns Mean

The first of the four columns, labeled "Clear," is of special significance. This means in our judgment every statement answered in the first column is a clear symptom of childhood sexual violation. If properly and honestly answered, it can directly and clearly be attributed to no other thing. On this test most people who have in fact been violated, whether the abuse is known or unknown, will mark at least four symptoms in the Clear column. Many respondents, however, will mark eight, ten, fourteen, or more responses, which only further serve to confirm what the survey is revealing. Marking three or fewer *does not mean no violation has occurred*. Even only one response in this column would need to be evaluated by someone who is knowledgeable about these symptoms in order to gain a clearer understanding.

We cannot overemphasize the importance of understanding the symptoms and identifying the real root cause of the problems. Anything less will probably mean putting spiritual or even psychological band-aids over deep chasms of unknown and unexplained pain and dysfunction. We have seen over and over again the joyous results when the real issues are courageously faced and dealt with, and true and rapid healing takes place.

Responses in the second column are "Strong" indicators that abuse took place. These responses often are given by victims of childhood abuse, but causes of these symptoms could also come from other sources. They are important responses to consider, but not as clear an indication of abuse as responses in the Clear column.

Similarly, responses in the third column, "Possible," are possible indicators that your wife was sexually interfered with during childhood. But problems indicated by these responses are more likely to have come from nonsexual sources, including such things as rejection.

Responses in the fourth column, "Group," are indications that the abuse perpetrated against your wife was done by a group or at least by more than one violator. Usually someone who checks several responses in the fourth column also marks several first-column items.

For further understanding of these symptoms and what they mean, we would suggest reading chapter 11 of our book, *Get a Life Without the Strife,* which gives a detailed analysis of the symptoms and the possible responses.

Reactions to the Survey Results

Once you have discovered the root cause of your wife's problems you can begin to apply the remedy. As you both look at the scores (the number of symptoms your wife has acknowledged about herself), one or both of you may have felt one of the typical reactions listed here. Each of you put your own mark in front of the one with which you most closely identify.

_____ 1. I've always wondered about that. Maybe now we can get to the bottom of our problems.

_____ 2. Is this possible? I can't believe this could have happened.

_____ 3. This is impossible! I (my wife) was raised in a good Christian home. My (her) father would never have done such a thing.

_____ 4. If it's true, I don't want to know. I'm afraid I couldn't handle it.

Which one is closest to your feelings? The first response is the healthiest. It indicates acceptance; the second indicates doubt, the third indicates denial, and the fourth indicates fear. If twelve or more responses were marked on the entire survey and your response was number 2, 3, or 4, begin praying for God to remove your blinders of doubt, denial, or fear. Then take a healthy second look at what the survey may be trying to tell you. Any symptoms checked in the first (Clear) column must be treated as significant. The certainty of abuse increases with the number of symptoms. Remember the statistics:

- Three out of four women have significant symptoms of victimization.
- One out of four acknowledges or is aware of it.
- Two out of four have no knowledge of it but do have the symptoms. The violation has been suppressed into the unconscious or unknown.[2]

This is a good time to share the three most consistent conclusions I've learned from my own study, my work with other victims of childhood abuse, and my personal experiences. I've summarized these conclusions as three basic axioms that turn out to be true in almost every case of childhood sexual victimization. Keep these principles in mind as you seek understanding of this destructive force:

Basic Axiom #1. Most childhood victimization begins between the ages of three and five, when a child is most defenseless and most trusting, not after age ten as many people suspect. A child violated at ten who does little or nothing to resist is a clear indication that this may not be the first time abuse has occurred. By the ages of eight, nine, ten, and older, a child's natural, God-given defense mechanisms are becoming stronger and stronger and, in general, she will do the best of her increasing ability to protect herself.

Basic Axiom #2: Only victims are apt to become victimizers. Lawrence in Sydney, Australia, who dropped my bombshell on me, is a typical example. A convicted child molester, he had been molested, himself, as a child.

Basic Axiom #3: Victims tend to marry victims. Is this significant to you? It could be. If your wife showed clear symptoms of childhood violation on the survey and is, or was, therefore an emotionally hurting person, what are the possibilities for her husband?

If you and your wife have now discovered that there must be repressed abuse buried deep inside her conscious awareness, you have taken one gigantic step forward. It becomes an even greater achievement if you are both willing to say, "Now that we have some idea of what the real root of our strife and unhappiness is, we are ready to get to work cleaning out the trash. We're willing to do whatever we have to do to become whole again. We are going to work on this together because it is affecting us together."

How do you start this work?

1. Talk about it whenever both of you feel like you want to.

2. Begin reading the best books available to give you insight and understanding. See Star Lysandra Cole's recommendations at the end of chapter 8.

3. If needed, find an understanding and knowledgeable Christian counselor or pastor who can effectively guide you. In addition to a detailed analysis of the test results, *Get a Life Without the Strife* also has a very helpful chapter on finding and working with a counselor.

4. Recognize that the *work* of healing means just that. It will require effort and energy. There is no magical cure.

5. Three things are needed in never-ceasing abundance: patience, tenderness, and perseverance. Your ability to demonstrate liberal doses of patience and tenderness to your wife will have a profound impact on her ability to heal.

6. Remember that healing is a journey, not an event. It will take time, tolerance, and togetherness for both of you. The steps of successful healing are clearly outlined in my book, *The Promise of Healing* (originally published as *The Promise of Restoration*, reprinted by Thomas Nelson in 1994 as *The Promise of Healing*). Hundreds—perhaps thousands—of people have told us it helped them find freedom from childhood victimization. Work on it together.

In chapter 11 I'll suggest some practical steps you can take to help restore physical intimacy to your marriage during your healing journey.

A Second Barrier to Marital Intimacy

While we believe childhood sexual victimization is the most common cause of problems with marital intimacy, there are two more obstacles that are often linked to this situation. The first has to do with the husband's irresponsibility and his failure to meet his wife's emotional needs. I saw an example of this in a couple who came to us during one of our seminars in Ohio.

Margie had come to us for help in resolving the problems she and her husband were having. Terry was her second husband, and they had been married ten years. Terry sold life insurance, but sometimes he didn't go in to work. Other times he went to the office and made calls but didn't actually go out to see anyone. Margie said she loved Terry but she was frustrated because she could never depend on him.

I invited her to bring Terry in to talk with me, and Margie did. We met privately for more than an hour on the last day of the seminar. Terry was a most pleasant Phlegmatic, neither defensive nor in denial. I gave the two of them some steps I knew from experience would be instrumental in bringing healing to them individually and to the family as a whole. Then I continued to have telephone contact with both of them over the next year. I was disappointed that neither of them was effectively following the pathway I had marked for them. As a result little progress was made in their relationship. Terry supported the family when he could. The rest of the time Margie had to rely on the dwindling remains of an insurance settlement.

One day Margie called me, very upset. Terry had paid their rent with a check that bounced. When she got the returned-check notice in the mail she called him at work, and he admitted there was no money in the account but he had hoped maybe some would come in to cover it. Even worse, he said he had also written checks on this account to pay the electricity and phone bills, so those checks would be returned also. At least this time he had told the truth, Margie said; on too many other similar occasions he had lied to avoid the issue. Margie was fed up; she simply couldn't trust him anymore. To make matters worse, she said, he had come home that day, wanting her to make love to him. "I love him, but I can't make love with him. Not when he doesn't seem to care anything about my welfare," she said. "He only seems to be thinking of himself and his own sexual needs. I am so mad at him. I can't put any stock in anything he tells me. He's so irresponsible and he's not communicating honestly with me about our problems."

Fortunately, Terry and Margie are now in the Christian counseling I recommended to them. Margie is starting to get serious about her life and what she needs to do to get it under control. Terry, on the other hand, hasn't made much progress. He's not defensive; he's not in denial. But he's not yet willing to make the consistent effort necessary to get his own life back on track. Yet he wants his wife to be responsive to his needs.

Recently when we were discussing this kind of problem with a friend of ours, she said with a wry smile, "The brain is the biggest sex organ there is. Women can't get into sex with their husbands until conflict is resolved and their minds are put at ease."

The second common barrier to marital intimacy, then, is the irresponsible husband who fails to fulfill his marital roles and is insensitive to his wife's emotional needs. Are you like Terry? Has your wife learned she cannot rely on you? Have you allowed your own problems to make you irresponsible, at least to your wife? Or are you a husband who has demonstrated over the years that your wife can depend on you and have confidence that you will protect her and provide for her? When our wives learn they can trust us emotionally then they can respond to us intimately.

Some of us men need to wake up and look at ourselves. If you think your wife may question whether you are responsible and whether she can trust you emotionally, ask her. Sit down and talk about the things in your relationship that are important to her. Find out from her how you can do a better job of meeting her needs, of being the husband she can depend on. You may then be surprised to find that she is able to more easily give herself to you intimately. If you need help in starting this dialogue, read the chapter titled "How Do I Communicate?" in our book, *Get a Life Without the Strife*. The Communication in Marriage Survey in that chapter has also helped many couples effectively focus on those thorny areas that are difficult to discuss.

The Third Barrier to Marital Intimacy

Husbands who physically or emotionally abuse their wives can have little expectation of ever experiencing the warmth of intimacy that is every couple's desire. Those abusive men are robbing not only themselves but also their wives of the very best God intended for them.

If you have ever hit your wife in anger you have physically abused her. You have pushed her away from you and shown her she can't trust you. The husband's role is to protect his wife. Who is to protect her from her protector? Who will step in to keep her safe if we become physically abusive? Would you stand by and allow someone else to hit her? Of course not! Virtually every one of us would lay our lives on the line without a moment's hesitation to protect the woman God gave us! Yet in too many homes—including Christian homes—it is the husband who is threatening the wife's safety.

Even yelling or raising your voice in anger may be construed to be emotional abuse of your wife. Criticizing or putting your wife down publicly or even in the privacy of your own home can be both devastating and demoralizing to her. We must try to make every word we speak to our wives encouraging and edifying. Ephesians 4:29 tells us, "Let no corrupt communication proceed out of your mouth, but that which is good to the use of edifying, that it may minister grace unto the hearers." When was the last time the words you said to your wife, or the way you said them, did not meet that test? We can reduce that scripture to just three little words: "Is it edifying?" Check yourself to see if every word that comes out of your mouth meets that requirement. You may be amazed to realize how easy it is to fail!

If you recognize that you frequently say things to your wife that make her feel stupid, unappreciated, or worthless, frankly admit to yourself now that you are emotionally abusing her. Acknowledging this as fact is the first step to changing and restoring a healthy relationship. The second step is to examine yourself to find out why you are acting the way you do. Too often we men are unwilling to do this. It's much easier to blame our partner. "If only she would change, I could be happy," we insist. "There's nothing wrong with me. She's the one who causes all the problems." These are the typical male reactions. Those were the things I used to say. But not anymore. I was finally forced to look at myself to see where my abusive patterns came from. And when I found out I began to work on changing myself and accepting Florence just the way she was. I quit trying to improve her so I could be happy. I started encouraging her and edifying her. I started to treat her as a fragile flower. I let her know how valuable and important she was to me. It took time. I had spent so many years tearing her down because of my own insecurities, it was difficult for her to regain her trust in me; it took time for her bruised emotions to heal. Yes, it took time, effort, and patience, but the results are worth it! Today we are best friends and can't imagine life apart from each other.

Wake up! Take a good look at yourself and your marriage. Is one of these barriers to intimacy at work in your home? If it is, my message to you is: Work on it. Don't give up. If your wife wants to enjoy intimacy with you but is unable to give herself to you in this way, remember: *There is a reason.* The root cause may lie in her childhood hurts, or it may be due to your irresponsibility or your physical or emotional abuse. Invite the Lord to work His healing in your marriage. Ask Him to help you face your problem, trace its source, and then, by His grace, erase it.

10

VICTIMS TEND TO MARRY VICTIMS

I was surprised when Betsy stepped up to the book table at a recent church conference and asked,"Fred, is there any chance you could meet with Linden and me before you and Florence leave for home?"

Betsy and her husband, Linden, an associate pastor at the church, had picked us up at the airport when we arrived in Orlando. They were both vibrant, outgoing, and obviously very much in love. Florence and I quickly came to enjoy this attractive young married couple. As I considered what they could want to discuss with me, I decided it was probably the problems Betsy had said her parents were struggling with at that time.

But I was wrong. Very wrong.

When we met at the agreed-upon time I saw before me two deeply committed Christians without any apparent problems. They seemed loving and caring toward each other, and I already knew that Sanguine Linden was enthusiastic about the successful ministry he was developing with the young people at the church.

I learned in the next minute that they were also very open about talking of what was on their minds. Betsy immediately began by saying, "Fred, the reason we wanted to see you is that, even though Linden and

I are very much in love and very happy in our marriage, I am not able to give myself sexually to him as I want to do. I don't know why. I thought maybe you could help us."

While I was surprised to hear this was *their* problem, I wasn't surprised by the problem, itself. As the previous chapter suggested, this is not an uncommon situation. Literally hundreds of other couples have come to me with the same dilemma in dozens of other cities around the world. Since we are helpers from out of town people feel comfortable sharing with us the facts about themselves that they couldn't risk saying to someone at home. They know we'll fly away in a day or two, taking with us their confidentialities.

"Well, let's begin by having you take this simple survey," I said, handing them copies of the Survey of Emotions and Experiences. (For the women's version of this survey, see chapter 9. The men's version is at the end of this chapter.) "This will tell us quickly what the roots of the problem may or may not be."

As they worked on the survey, I considered two of the facts I've learned from experience: First, the problem Betsy described often stemmed from childhood sexual victimization. But I knew Betsy's parents. They were recognized leaders in the church, and they were the ones who had invited us there. Knowing this, I dreaded how this could turn out, but Betsy and Linden had come to me for help and I was committed to doing all I could for them. The consequences we would have to leave to the Lord.

And then there was the second probability to consider: Victims tend to marry victims.

It took only a few minutes for the couple to finish the surveys. I looked at Betsy's responses first. She had checked only three symptoms: one clear, one strong, and one possible. This was surprising—the most minute indication of victimization when, from her presenting problem, I expected several symptoms. *Well*, I thought, *maybe this is the exception to the rule.* Then I looked at Linden's responses. He had checked five in the first column of clear symptoms and three in each of the next two, for a total of eleven. Not an overwhelming case, perhaps, but clear enough.

I explained to both of them that the purpose of the survey was to determine the possibility of some form of sexual violation in their childhoods. Linden had acknowledged on his survey some problems with pornography but explained that he had pretty much gained a victory over it. I told Linden that based on what he was saying about himself on the survey there was a very strong possibility that someone had done something to him as a child. He was in no way defensive or in denial, but he said if it had happened he had no knowledge of it. "If it did happen," he added, "how can I find out?"

I reminded Linden that the Lord knew every day of his life since he was conceived in his mother's womb. If he wanted to know, we would simply have to ask the One who already knows. I explained how the Lord could reveal the truth through prayer for memory retrieval.

Linden wanted to know.

But it was Betsy who had come with the problem. We looked at her survey again. I asked her about the only symptom she had checked in the first "Clear" column: "Early-childhood masturbation (before age ten)." She clearly remembered that as early as age seven, she would frequently rub herself back and forth on the corner of the hassock in the living room.

It was really unusual to have only one clear symptom, but this was a very clear one. Little girls, according to God's design for the healthy development of their body, mind, and emotions, should not be having sexual feelings until about the age of puberty. Seven was way too early, unless . . . unless somehow her natural, God-given sexuality had been inappropriately awakened by something that had been done to her.

Both Betsy and Linden wanted to know what was interfering with their love relationship. Could I pray with them now? they asked. Our normal procedure before praying for memories includes a minimum of two weeks of spiritual and emotional preparation consisting of prayer and reading. But they were both anxious to know, and I felt led to pray with them then. Since Linden had the clearer symptoms we agreed to seek his memories first, and we set a time two days later for Betsy, giving her some time to prepare. She shared the concerns that had already occurred to me. What if it was her father, with whom she had a very close relationship? I shared her apprehension. Her father was my friend. How would I handle the revelation? The two days before Betsy's session would give me time to go to the Lord with these questions.

Tracing the Roots of the Problem

As Linden's memory retrieval began, he prayed first; then I prayed, asking the Lord Jesus to reveal the truth. Betsy supported us in silent prayer. Within only a few seconds Linden saw himself at the camp he had attended when he was seven. He was in the cabin and could see everything quite clearly. There didn't seem to be anyone else in there. Then he noticed someone lying on the bunk to the right. It was the counselor. His pants were open; he was exposed. Little Linden was lured over to give him oral sex. Linden opened his eyes. He was amazed. His prayer had been answered that quickly. He knew it was true. He also knew his heavenly Father would not give him a stone when he asked for bread. As he thought more about it, so many other things began to make sense.

We prayed again for the Lord to minister healing to Linden, and He did. Both Betsy and Linden were amazed at the Lord's swift revelation. This was totally new to Linden. He had no previous conscious knowledge of this incident. But he walked out of that room newly released and set free. Before they left that Sunday, I referred them to Philippians 1:6 and reminded Linden how important it would be for him to continue the journey of healing so God could continue the work He and Linden had begun. The most important part of this journey, I told him, was daily written prayer.

Tuesday afternoon came, and Betsy and Linden were back. Having witnessed what God had done for her husband, Betsy was eager to know the truth about her own childhood. Now she wanted the same for herself. "But what will I do if it's my dad? How will I handle that?" she asked. I had no clear answers for her except to remind her, "We don't know it's your dad, so we don't have to deal with that question at the moment." Nevertheless, she wanted to know the truth, no matter who might be involved.

Once again we prayed, as we had done on Sunday with Linden. As Betsy prayed, the Lord took her to her home when she was four years old. She had no conscious knowledge of the memory she saw next. She was in the front bedroom of her home, looking back at the door. Someone, a man, was standing there. He came in the room, went over to the bed, and called little Betsy over. The man was "Grampie," her grandfather. He exposed himself and made little Betsy perform the same sex act for him that Linden had been talked into doing for the camp counselor. Betsy could hardly believe it, and yet she, too, knew that it was true. She could not have made it up; there were too many precise details that she knew were true. Linden knew it was true as well. The Lord then came to Betsy in that memory and ministered His healing to her in a way that was similar to how He had come to Linden. That was surely real! Betsy was stunned but also relieved that the victimizer hadn't been her father.

Betsy called her parents that night to ask some questions about the house in her memory. Her mother not only described the house and the front bedroom just as Betsy had seen it, but also told her that during those years both of her parents had worked during the day and Grampie often came over to babysit little Betsy! That also explained why no one else was at home. If Betsy had any doubts they were dispelled by her mother's confirmation!

Was it necessary, was it valuable, for Betsy and Linden to learn the truth about their childhood violations? How could this help them? Wouldn't they have been better off to leave well enough alone?

Remember this young couple were brave enough and open enough to acknowledge early on that they had a problem. These kinds of issues do not normally disappear by themselves. Instead, they tend to get worse. Betsy and Linden faced their trouble head-on. They traced the roots of their problems and, by God's grace, they erased them. Two days later when Linden drove me back to the airport for our departure, he joyfully shared that that very morning Betsy had wanted to make love and, as the Book of Genesis might describe it, "God saw that it was good." The Lord had already worked a miracle by bringing healing to their marriage.

Although the names and other identifying facts have been changed, this is the true story of two young people whose marital life was being affected by totally unknown acts that were committed against each of them in their childhoods. Now they were set free. Although I couldn't see at first how this situation would play out, my original ideas were confirmed: First, problems like Betsy's are often linked to childhood sexual abuse, and second, victims tend to marry victims. But the Lord Jesus can overcome these obstacles and bring healing, as He did for Betsy and Linden.

Jesus said, "I have come to heal the brokenhearted, to set the captive free" (paraphrase of Luke 4:18).

Applying These Principles to Your Own Life

Did your wife complete the Survey of Emotions and Experiences for Women included in the last chapter? Does she have symptoms or knowledge of childhood victimization? If the answer to this question is in any way yes, then what is the implication for you? If it is true that victims tend to marry victims, and your wife shows symptoms of childhood victimization, would you be willing to consider the possibility that *you* might also have been subjected to such things as a child? Remember the basic facts, 10 percent of all men are aware of childhood trauma, while another 50 percent have the same kinds of symptoms but no awareness of childhood abuse. Their memories have been totally repressed.

Are there issues or problems in your own life now that you would like to be free of? Remember Jesus said, "Ye shall know the truth, and the truth shall make you free" (John 8:32).

How many of the following issues apply to you? Check the ones that do.

_____ 1. Do your family members tend to be afraid of your anger and sometimes seem to avoid you?

____ 2. Do you have a tendency to feel sorry for yourself?

____ 3. Is there anything you feel afraid of and wonder why you're afraid of it and whether it's a normal thing for a man to fear?

____ 4. Do you sometimes think you're not worth much and that nobody really loves you?

____ 5. Have you ever been chased by something or someone in a dream?

____ 6. Do you sometimes have an obsessive focus on either the female or the male body?

____ 7. Would your wife or your family say that they think you have a tendency to be overly critical?

____ 8. Do you have a tendency to be very private about your feelings? Do you feel reluctant to share them with your wife?

____ 9. Would your wife say you are apt to be overly jealous of her?

____ 10. Do you sometimes find yourself doing something that you later hate yourself for having done—and realize you had almost no control to avoid doing it?

If you marked two or more of these questions you will probably find it very beneficial to take the time right now to go through the Survey of Emotions and Experiences for Men, which follows. Even if you only responded to one, or even none of the questions above, you may find the survey to be of interest to you. It may answer some questions that have already been rolling around in your mind. When answered accurately and honestly, it has proven to be more than 99 percent accurate in determining the possibility of repressed childhood trauma.

Was it important for your wife to know the truth? Then shouldn't it be important for you to know the truth about yourself too? This is where many men bog down. It's all right for their wives to deal with childhood issues that might be the root of their adult strife, but men are often unwilling to look at themselves objectively. Which kind of husband will you be? One who is willing to go forward or one who makes one of these excuses:

"That's in the past, it doesn't matter now."

"I don't have the time."

"Whatever might have happened, it's all covered by Jesus's blood—forgiven and forgotten. There's no need to dig into that stuff."

"I'm just not interested."

"I've got enough problems on my mind, I couldn't deal with that now."
Here is the survey. I urge you to make the effort to examine yourself
so that if anything has been stolen from your emotional life or your marriage, you will be able to give God the opportunity to restore it to you.

Survey of Emotions and Experiences
For Men

Check each line that applies or *ever has applied* to you. Note that the
blank for each statement falls under one of four column headings, which
are explained in the "Scoring the Survey" section in chapter 9, beginning on page 98. Leave blank any statements that do not apply or you
are not sure of.

	Clear	Strong	Possible	Group
1. Affairs during marriage			___	
2. Afraid of big or black dogs				___
3. Alcoholic parent		___		
4. Being chased in dreams	___			
5. Brother or sister molested as a child	___			
6. Candles in dreams				___
7. Childhood "bad houses" or "bad rooms"	___			
8. Childhood depression			___	
9. Downcast looks as a child	___			
10. Dreams of snakes	___			
11. Early-childhood anger	___			
12. Early-childhood masturbation (before age ten)	___			
13. Emotionally abused as child			___	
14. Emotions suppressed in childhood			___	
15. Fear of being alone	___			
16. Fear of knives				___

	Clear	Strong	Possible	Group
17. Feel unworthy of God's love	___			
18. Feeling "dirty"	___			
19. Fits of rage	___			
20. Flashbacks of sexual nature	___			
21. Frequent teenage masturbation	___			
22. Guilt feelings			___	
23. Hate Halloween				___
24. Hate homosexuals	___			
25. Hear chanting or laughing in dreams				___
26. Hide real feelings			___	
27. Lack of trust		___		
28. Low self-worth		___		
29. Marital sexual disinterest			___	
30. Memory gaps in childhood	___			
31. Migraine headaches	___			
32. Obsessive focus on breasts or vagina	___			
33. Panic attacks	___			
34. People wearing hoods or robes in dreams				___
35. Physically abused as child			___	
36. Poor teenage relationships			___	
37. Recurring bad dreams	___			
38. Rejection feelings			___	
39. Same-sex attraction	___			
40. Scared by bells, chimes, or gongs				___
41. Self-hatred	___			
42. Sexually abused or molested as child	___			

	Clear	Strong	Possible	Group
43. Sexual compulsions, i.e., magazines, videos	____			
44. Sometimes hear voices				____
45. Spiders in dreams	____			
46. Strange feelings about "the cross"				____
47. Struggle with holiness	____			
48. Suicidal feelings			____	
49. Teenage promiscuity			____	
50. Teenage sexual touching with boys	____			
51. Temptation to touch children sexually	____			
52. Tendency to overreact			____	
53. Tendency to look at others' penises	____			
54. Uncomfortable with nudity in marriage	____			
55. Uncontrollable anger		____		
56. Uncontrollable crying	____			
57. Undiagnosed pains and aches	____			
58. Unexplained fear of darkness				____
Your totals	____	____	____	____
Possible	25	10	13	10

Grand total (add all four column totals): ____

Note: This Survey of Emotions and Experiences for Men and the following scoring analysis are adapted from *Get a Life Without the Strife* by Fred and Florence Littauer (Thomas Nelson, 1993). All rights reserved. Used by permission, This form may be reproduced.

Add up your responses in each of the four columns and enter the score on the "Your totals" line (the numbers under each of the lines indicate the possible number for that column). Then add up your four column totals to get your grand total of responses.

Note: it really helps if you actually mark those statements that apply to you rather than "eyeballing" the lines and trying to remember how many you responded to in each column.

What is your total in the first, the "Clear," column? As in the survey for women in chapter 9, responses in this column are the most significant. If you have marked three or four of these symptoms in the first column, you have indicated a very strong possibility that you, too, were sexually interfered with as a child. The greater your number of marks, the more certain the likelihood, even if you have absolutely no such memory and don't even believe it is possible. Fewer than three responses in this column does not necessarily mean you are one of the fortunate ones who escaped. Remember that Betsy checked only one symptom in the first column and only three responses overall when she took the survey. Yet the Lord clearly gave her the memory of what her grandfather did to her. Only one or two marks in the first column could still be significant.

For further understanding of your survey results, go back and read the scoring explanations beginning on page 98 in chapter 9. Further clarification of the significance of these symptoms may be found in the chapter titled "How Can I Know If I Was Sexually Violated as a Child?" in our book, *Get a Life Without the Strife.*

You might want to turn back and reconsider those ten questions on page 112. Your survey results may begin to give you some understanding of why you answered yes to some of those questions.

A Personal Quest for Truth

What are your own conclusions about the survey you have just taken? Is there evidence of sexual violation in your own childhood? If your answer is yes, this may be one of the most significant steps you have taken in understanding yourself. It could help explain some of the common manifestations of boyhood sexual victimization that may be part of your adult life, such as chronic anger, chronic depression, sexual obsessions, or never having felt good about yourself or never achieving what you felt you should, to name just a few.

If you can honestly answer the survey with no symptoms, then you may be very grateful that you are one of the two out of five men who escaped violation during childhood. Nevertheless, the information you have considered and the time you have spent have not been wasted. First of all, you have learned more about yourself and you can be confident this is one area of your life you probably don't need to be concerned about. Second, we have found that God never wastes information. Soon (for many it happens within a week of taking the survey) some other man may casually mention some of his struggles to you. Then you will be able to recommend this resource as a way to help him deal with his own issues and begin his own healing journey.

For those of you who answered yes, even reluctantly, the next thing we strongly recommend is that you now begin your own personal quest for the truth. You can start by rereading the recommendations for women outlined in chapter 9. They are the same for men.

You cannot imagine the changes and opportunities that will be available to you when you have fully addressed these issues and received the cleansing and healing the Lord desires to give you. You cannot comprehend, until you have experienced it, how much more rewarding your life can be. You will be amazed at how much deeper and more meaningful your relationship with the Lord can be when nothing is blocking your spiritual growth. My own life and example are clear evidence of the changes a man can experience when he is willing to identify his problems, trace and face them, and by God's grace and with His help, erase them. I would like you to know and to have these blessings and benefits for your own life.

It is time for us men to wake up and see ourselves as others see us. It is time for us to step out and be the leaders in bringing the peace, the love, and the joy of our Lord to our homes. It is not something we can legislate or command; it is something we must demonstrate by making it a reality in our own lives.

Our responsibility for our families goes much deeper than merely earning a living so we can feed, house, and clothe them. Those are all important responsibilities, but there is much more. So much depends on how well we exert the special spiritual and emotional leadership that begins when we are honest with ourselves about how we are affecting the health and security of those who have entrusted their lives to us. For too long most of us, including myself, have said this is the woman's job.

When we are in obedience to God's role for us as men, as husbands, and as fathers, and when we stop blaming our wives for the struggles in our relationship and find and deal with our own part in any problems, then, and only then, can we begin to experience the peace, the power, and the purpose God intended for us when our Savior gave His life for us!

11

MARITAL INTIMACY DURING
THE HEALING JOURNEY

One thing you can be sure of, when there has been sexual victimization during childhood, there will be sexual problems in marriage. Whether the abuse was done to one or both spouses, childhood violation can seem to destroy the marital intimacy the husband and wife anticipated as they looked forward to a lifetime together. The effects of any form of sexual abuse on a child can be so devastating his or her sexuality may be grossly distorted throughout the rest of his or her life.*

I sometimes wonder if victimizers ever consider just how much they are damaging a child as they force him or her to satisfy their compulsive urges. I wonder if that German housekeeper had any idea how her actions would impact my adult life in so many different ways. Did Betsy's grandfather ever realize for one moment that he was robbing his precious granddaughter of her right to sexual fulfillment in her future marriage? The answer is probably that these perpetrators never gave it a moment's thought. If

---

* I am deeply indebted to Star Lysandra Cole for her research and analysis, upon which this chapter is based, and for her unstinting selflessness to permit me to draw upon her insight.

they did, they probably convinced themselves the child would never remember or that it wouldn't hurt the child or that the child needed to learn about sexual things.

While we consider this person's actions we must also understand that important axiom: Virtually every victimizer was victimized as a child. The sexuality of a violated child can become so disrupted that in adulthood he or she may feel the need for a child to satisfy the distorted sexual cravings. (But this does *not* mean that every victim becomes a victimizer!) Healthy men and women do not even entertain the thought of inappropriate sexual activity with a defenseless child.

But there is hope for the wife or the husband who has suffered this trauma in childhood. If we believe in the power of the risen Lord to bring healing, then we know there is not only hope, but change and healing as well. This healing is a process, however, not an event. Everyone has a different personality, and anyone who has been violated experiences different struggles. The way individuals deal with their specific issues differs from person to person. Each case of victimization is different, and each instance of healing will be different. Not everyone experiences the sudden release Betsy did (and even Betsy will need time to continue working prayerfully through all the emotional issues the revelation unleashed).

There are steps you can take to help your wife and yourself as you work through your respective healing journeys. First, recognize that struggles with marital intimacy are common among couples when one or both have suffered childhood abuse. You would surely be amazed if you knew how many couples have to deal with these issues. You are not alone. If 60 percent of men and 75 percent of women were victimized during childhood, the figures for couples who are now confused and searching for answers must be equally high!

For women who have been traumatically violated (differing from those who have been seductively violated), it is usually very difficult or even impossible for them to respond to their husbands. Their lack of feeling becomes even more confusing when they have no knowledge of any abuse. Like Betsy, they just can't understand why they can't be relaxed and free. They tend to freeze or turn away or claim to have a headache or feel too tired. As a result their husbands are apt to feel unwanted, unloved, and rejected. Unless these husbands and wives are able to discuss their feelings with each other, the husbands will too easily be tempted to find someone else to meet their needs. They become vulnerable, and satan's plan for destruction of the home moves another step forward.

When the husbands are the ones who have been violated, the usual pattern is just the reverse of this. Their need for sex often becomes compulsive and excessive, and they are apt to be obsessive about sexual things. And since victims tend to marry victims, the sexually driven man is often married to a woman who was victimized as a child and is, as a result, sexually unresponsive as an adult.

While this pattern describes the typical adult manifestation of childhood abuse, the opposite can also occur: Because of the nature of their violation, some men have little to no interest in sex and may have married a victim who was seductively and frequently violated in her childhood and as an adult has a craving for sex.

If these issues relate to you, it is important for you to see that you are not abnormal, defective, or inadequate, or that your marriage is hopeless. But to achieve resolution and restoration it is essential that each day you prayerfully ask the Lord to strengthen your compassion, patience, and understanding. We men sometimes do fairly well with the compassion and understanding part, at least for a while. It's in the area of patience that we need extra help!

Suggestions for Husbands

Without knowing it, you may be the catalyst that catapults your wife emotionally into the past. Something as simple as whether you showered, shaved, or brushed your teeth before coming to bed may trigger long-repressed feelings that even your wife doesn't understand. Odors and smells are often powerful triggers that alert the body or the emotions to fear or shame or the need for protection. They may replicate something your wife had to endure as a child. Do not be surprised if your wife reacts to certain colognes, aftershaves, or shaving creams but has no idea why. Try to be sensitive to her feelings. Learn what she is and is not comfortable with. Do not push her or "demand your rights" at any time when she is not comfortable. Anything less may be a revictimization to her, and you then are no better to her emotionally than the person who hurt her.

Treat her like a precious, fragile flower and she will do the very best for you she can. Remember that a woman's basic desire is to please her husband. God created her that way. She is happiest when she knows she can and is appreciated by her man. Don't take anything for granted, and let her know how much you appreciate her and everything she tries to do for you.

Body language, before and while you are in bed, can make her sense that something will be physically or emotionally painful. Make sure the way you approach her is comfortable and nonthreatening for her. Certain physical positions can recreate a scene of panic from her childhood.

If she suddenly becomes hysterical and pushes you away, it's not you she's rejecting. She is emotionally reacting to a repressed body memory. Touching her in certain places or in certain ways may trigger the feelings of what happened to her years before when she was totally out of control and at the mercy of the violator, who probably didn't show any! It is not unusual for a wife to not want her husband to lie on top of her. This recreates the smothered and stifling feelings she endured when someone five to eight times her weight and size was on top of her. Respect your wife's feelings and her needs. Never ask her to do anything she considers a violation of her feelings or femininity.

While your wife may be receiving messages that signal danger and fear, you may be receiving messages that are diametrically opposite to where her heart and emotions are. It would be normal for the husband to be feeling *She doesn't really love me . . . I'm only important to her as a meal ticket . . . She's just using me . . . I'm a rotten lover . . . There's something wrong with me . . . She's using sex as a weapon to control me . . . If I had better technique she'd enjoy it.* NONE of these messages are usually true, but without understanding it's easy to see how they could be perceived by a frustrated husband.

Coupled with all the many other dynamics resulting from abuse, your wife may also be wrestling with feelings of doubt, shame, and guilt because she is not able to make love with her husband and doesn't understand why. She may be wrestling with fear and frustration of her own. Most women and many men who have been violated feel that they are dirty, unacceptable, and unworthy of God's love. Sometimes it is impossible for them to accept the Fatherhood of God when their violator was a father figure.

Five Things Your Wife Needs from You

Your wife needs at least five things from you in the area of intimacy as she is learning about and dealing with her traumatic childhood issues. Give her these things, but remember that she must deal with her own pain in her own way as the Lord leads her. Any attempts to apply pressure or foster your own ideas upon her will inevitably prove to be counterproductive.

Control. If she has been violated she has never had the right to control her own body or her physical contact with others. She's never had the opportunity to learn that intimacy can feel safe and good. Instead, she has always felt controlled, manipulated, deceived, or forced to do things against her will. She needs the freedom to choose.

Safety. Your wife needs to learn to feel safe with you. You must be her shining white knight, her protector. She's never ever had one before. She must be able to trust that you will never push her beyond where she feels comfortable. She must know that you are only thinking about her needs and desires, that you put her feelings ahead of your own. Then she may be able to take a few small risks. If she feels safe during these small risks, she may be able to risk a further step. Remember that victimizers of children use manipulation, deception, threats, and rewards. Be sure you do not do the same! Touch her only in ways you already know are safe and acceptable to her. Be reminded, however, that "it is a woman's prerogative to change her mind!" What was safe last time may not be safe today. Above all else, don't betray her trust!

Security. Your wife desperately needs to know she is loved for *who* she is, not for what she can *do* for you. She needs to be valued and appreciated. She needs to know you will not get angry or sulk when she is unable to be responsive to you. This will be very difficult for you if you have been victimized as well, for rejection virtually always accompanies the emotional pain caused by sexual abuse. But expressing your own rejection feelings to her at this point will make her feel rejected anew, just when she is striving to heal in that area. You said you wanted to be the leader of your family and your household? This may be the battleground where your abilities will be put to their sternest test!

Patience. Your wife needs a husband who will be patient with her. In all likelihood no one has ever been patient with her before. Victimizers typically use their victims to their satisfaction then dismiss them like a bothersome puppy when their needs are satisfied. Remember that the healing process will take time; there will be setbacks and disappointments. Expect them, and learn to rise above them. When they do happen, be the encourager. Help your wife to believe in herself once again. Try to remember what you no doubt already know, that women tend to function on the basis of feelings. Men generally function on the basis of facts and rationale. That's why it is so hard for us to comprehend a woman's feelings. We need to keep trying until we do understand.

Tenderness. Your wife will need all the tenderness you can give her as she goes through the healing process. Your gentleness will help her learn to feel in control, safe and secure.

These five needs represent a big order. Can you fill it? Probably not in your own strength; this is more than most men could do on their own. There is probably only one way you will be able to accomplish this task and give to your wife what she needs from you. That is to come to the Lord Jesus each day in prayer, asking Him to do for you what you can't do by yourself. Ask Him to put His nature in you each day so you will be able to do what would normally be impossible for you. If you will ask Him, He will give you these desires of your heart for they are consistent with His desires for you and your wife. Never ask Him to change your wife so that she can fill your needs. That would be self-focused, and that's not the way the Lord works. He wants you to be Christ-focused so you can enjoy perfect peace (Isa. 26:3).

Specific Ways You Can Help Your Wife

So far we've talked about intangible ways you can help your wife on her journey to recovery. Now let's get down to specifics. Here are some practical suggestions for things you can do to ease the way for her.

Make the bedroom as emotionally and physically safe for your wife as you possibly can. Make it a refuge, a safe haven for her. Let her know she can look forward to going to the bed as a place of safety and protection. By both your words and your actions, assure her that in bed she can comfortably nestle in your strong arms without any concern that you will expect more from her than she is comfortable with or ready for. You may need to help her refocus her feelings a full 180 degrees from seeing the bed as place of fear and danger to place of love and protection.

Talk and communicate openly about your own emotions and feelings. Your willingness to talk about how you feel may give her "permission" to share with you how she feels. Both of you should be willing to discuss "boundary issues." It may be very helpful to put your understandings and agreements in writing. This would eliminate future confusion when one of you forgets what you agreed to.

Sometimes sexual issues are the most difficult to talk about openly and honestly. The reason is usually that one or both of you have been taught by past experiences and failures that you can't say what you feel because the results are too traumatic. Only recently has Florence learned that I will not get upset or try to "prove her wrong" when she tries to share her feelings with me. It took a long time for her to learn to overturn and heal her past conditioning to my earlier responses, which were often accompanied with anger. Remember to always practice the two basics of healthy marital communications. These two simple ground rules will help you significantly to grow in all your areas of communicating with each other:

- **No interrupting.** When you are ready to discuss feelings you should first set this essential ground rule, that neither of you will interrupt while the other is speaking. Since both of you will break this important agreement from time to time, you must also agree that the person who is interrupted always has the right to say, "Wait a minute. You interrupted me. Let me finish."

- **No "you-messages."** A "you-message" attacks or blames the other person for your own feelings. A simple example would be, "You always make me angry when you talk too long on the phone." This kind of a remark places the blame for your anger on your wife instead of maturely accepting responsibility for your own feelings or actions. You-messages can also back her into a position where she feels she has to defend herself; they can attack her sense of self-worth and personal integrity. She may have thought (correctly) that she had every right to talk on the phone as long as she did. A better way to have communicated the same message would have been to say, "Honey, I was waiting to use the phone when you were talking to Mary. I'm sorry I got upset; I should have let you know." In this non-attacking "I-message," you are giving your wife the opportunity to apologize for not thinking of you, rather than forcing her to defend her rights.

Pray together before coming together. The union of a husband and wife is the most profound experience of being one in Christ. Invite the Holy Spirit to send ministering angels to help you and your wife and guardian angels to do battle and protect you against the enemy's interference. Once again, you be the leader in your spiritual communion with the Lord. Don't pray that your wife will be what you want her to be. It is all too easy to use prayer to express your needs or feelings to your wife. This kind of manipulation may destroy any oneness for the moment. Prayer is between you and your Father in heaven. Pray that you will be the tender and considerate husband and lover your wife desires. This will bless her as she comes before the Father with you.

Respect your wife, and treat her as you want to be treated. Your wife has feelings and needs just as you do. But hers will most likely be very different from yours. As God makes you able, put her needs ahead of your own. "Be devoted to one another in brotherly love; give preference to one another in honor" (Rom. 12:10 NASB). "Do nothing from selfishness or empty conceit, but with humility . . . let each of you regard one another as more important than himself; do not merely look out for your own personal interests" (Phil. 2:3–4 NASB).

Look at those verses again. Over and over again the Bible tells us to put others' needs ahead of our own, and that includes our wife's needs. When you do, she will know you are treating her with respect; she will feel like a precious, fragile flower who knows you will protect her from every storm.

By following these steps and working together through the healing process, you will help your wife become able to enjoy—and even initiate—intimacy. Then you will know the Lord has truly redeemed the "years the locusts have eaten." Do you believe in miracles?

Sharing Your Needs with Your Wife

While you are helping your wife work through her journey to restoration, there are things she can do to help you as well. You will have some emotions and needs you have to deal with, and one of these needs is to share these feelings with your wife and ask for her understanding and help.

From experience in working with hundreds of couples, I know what many of these needs and feelings will be; they are discussed in the paragraphs that follow. Use these guidelines as a nonthreatening way to let your wife know what you are going through and what your needs are. If you present them carefully and without demands, she will not perceive these feelings as an attack on her or as evidence of your dissatisfaction with her. Add any additional feelings of your own.

If you were also abused as a child, remind your wife that many of your needs occur because feelings of rejection are typically so closely intertwined with the emotions caused by childhood violation. Remind her that honesty is essential if your marriage is to survive this process. But both of you should remember that honesty must be tempered with tenderness. Carefully share the things you know your wife can hear without feeling emotional pain, but for now avoid anything that will be destructive to her, even if it's true.

Reassurance. We all need to know we are loved and cherished. Honestly share with your wife what you desire, what your hopes are, and what you fear. Let your wife know you need to feel needed and wanted, that there are other ways besides sexual intimacy that she can use to communicate her feelings to let you know you are appreciated and valued as a husband. Her desire to lie close to you in bed without your initiating sex will reassure you that she appreciates your protective strength.

Acknowledgment. You need your wife to recognize your God-given desire to meet her needs to be sheltered, protected, and defended. She must allow you to be her comforter, to hold her, to help her, to allow you to be angry about what was done to her. You need to be able to cry with her, always returning to the confidence that the Lord will bring complete healing to both of you. She needs to allow you to share her deepest hurts, and you can only do that if she is willing to be vulnerable with you and let you know what she is feeling inside. If she doesn't feel she can do this, she needs to tell you why. If it's because she fears your reactions, ask her to help you understand what you do that troubles her. If it's because of her feelings of shame or guilt over what occurred, encourage her to let you help her through these feelings, exchanging those long-held lies for the everlasting truth of God's forgiveness and cleansing. She needs to show you how to help her, and then she needs to let you help! Only then can you build a relationship of mutual interdependence and respect.

Comfort. As the husband of a wife who was abused during childhood you are the secondary victim, and you have pain also. You have pain for what was stolen from you: your wife's wholeness, her undefiled love and trust, her freedom to give to you what is rightfully yours. You, too, need comfort. Your wife should recognize that she is the one who must provide the understanding and comfort for the hurts you are feeling. Her inability or unwillingness to do this makes you vulnerable to satan's attacks. He roams about like a roaring lion looking for someone he may devour!

Your responses to the Survey of Emotions and Experiences may have revealed that you, too, were victimized during your childhood. This may be underscored for you by the axiom that victims tend to marry victims—and you are married to a victim! If this is the case, you may be dealing with your own repressed emotions that are now surging to the surface. Your wife may even trigger the pain from your own past. If so, discuss these issues and feelings with her. Work diligently together to create an environment of trust and safety for both of you. Do everything you can to eliminate emotionally threatening situations and reactions. Support each other, encourage each other, share with each other. The very best condition for rapid recovery is when both husband and wife are working together individually and for each other. The Lord Jesus is already your Counselor (Isa. 6:9). You can be each other's therapist. "Therefore comfort one another with these words" (1 Thess. 4:18 NASB).

Physical contact. Until your wife is comfortable and ready for physical intimacy, she should be encouraged to make every effort to communicate love, caring, and warmth in nonteasing, nonsexual physical contact. A spontaneous hug, a snuggle, reaching out to hold hands, a touch when walking past, a kiss, or a backrub are just some of the ways she can help you with what you need. If the two of you have already established your healthy boundaries and mutual understanding, you will not misconstrue these actions as signals for more than your wife is ready for.

Your wife should work prayerfully to have sexual contact with you whenever she is able and in whatever manner she is able. Both of you must understand that your wife should never withhold sexual contact from you as a weapon or tool of manipulation. At the same time you must understand that she cannot be the warm, responsive wife you desire if you have been abusive in any way to her. *Don't even think about it!*

And now, a final word of caution for you: If you believe God can heal this area of your marriage and you desire Him to do it, never—repeat *never*—demand your scriptural rights of your wife or force yourself on her. You may win one self-centered contest, but you will destroy everything you have been working toward. Your wife will be victimized all over again, but this time you will be the victimizer!

12

DOES YOUR WIFE HAVE
AN ABUSIVE HUSBAND?

At a recent CLASS Seminar a young woman with an obvious sparkling Sanguine personality came up to Florence during one of the breaks. Florence had been talking about the vast number of hurting people in the church and the numerous ministry opportunities this presented for people who had answers and were able to articulate them. She mentioned that she and I were writing companion books, *Wake Up, Women!* and *Wake Up, Men!*, to help Christian men and women focus on some of the issues that were keeping them from moving forward in their lives.

The young woman, I'll call her Susan, said, "Well, I surely have a story if you'd like to use it!" Florence's antennae were immediately thrown into reception mode. She is always interested in valid personal experiences and is a master at using such stories to illustrate a point. When Florence and Susan met together later Susan shared this story.

A few years earlier a traveling evangelist had come to Susan's church in Canada. On about the third night of the week's meetings he introduced Susan to an attractive young man he had been ministering to in the church. The evangelist even set up their first date. Jason was immediately attracted to Susan and quickly proposed marriage. Caught up in the whirlwind courtship, Susan had little time to think through this idea or to analyze what was happening. She did have enough concern, however, to consult her pastor, who knew both of them very well. He knew Jason particularly well because he had been counseling with him for several months. This should have alerted Susan, but she was only twenty-five, was being swept off her feet, and she had never had anyone pay so much attention to her before. It felt good to have someone care for her, hold her. She had never really known what that was like before.

Her pastor assured Susan that all Jason needed was a "good woman," which Susan certainly was. He was sure Jason's problems would be resolved in a loving marriage relationship. So, only eight weeks after she met Jason, and with the pastor's encouragement and blessing, Susan and Jason were married.

Susan had looked forward to her wedding night; she had kept herself pure for whoever God would send to be her husband. But that night in the hotel Susan was hurt and disappointed that Jason kept himself glued to the basketball game on TV. He seemed to have forgotten she was there. *Oh well,* she thought, *maybe men aren't as romantic as women.* When the game was over, Jason got himself ready for bed. When Susan came to bed, Jason grabbed her, pulled her down, had what he wanted in a few minutes, then rolled over and went to sleep. Susan lay awake sobbing for hours. What had happened to her dream? What kind of a situation had she gotten herself into?

Susan quickly became aware that Jason did, indeed, have some problems, but she remembered what the pastor had said, that all he needed was a good woman to turn him around. As so many wives do when they find themselves in an abusive situation, she thought she could change Jason. She asked God to give her the patience to stick it out; divorce was unthinkable. Besides, she lived in a small town. What would the people, the church, and the pastor think? Susan prayed for Jason and she prayed for herself, asking God to give her strength. She asked God to love Jason through her.

But things were not getting better; they were getting worse. Jason refused to let her see any of her old friends. He insisted that she focus all her attention on him. Promising he would take care of her, Jason made Susan quit her job. Once she had no income of her own, he allowed her only ten dollars a week and made her account for every penny of it before she could have her next allotment. If Susan tried to question Jason about anything, he flew into a rage and told her he was the head of the house and it was her God-ordained duty to totally submit to his authority. He would make all the decisions, he said, and he always had Scripture verses to prove he was right.

The bedroom became a place of terror for Susan. Jason sometimes demanded sex two or three times a night and usually insisted Susan do things that were physically painful for her. He seemed to be completely unaware that she had any needs of her own. When she didn't satisfy him sufficiently or obey his command, he beat her.

One evening when he came home from work the neighbor's dog was lying in the driveway. Jason honked, but the dog didn't move fast enough. Susan watched in terror as Jason jumped from the car and mercilessly kicked the dog out of the way. Susan cried. She could feel for the poor dog. She had been kicked the same way.

Finally, in desperation, Susan went back to her pastor for help. He couldn't believe Jason would do the things she described, and he actually implied Susan was making it all up to get attention. He prayed with her and told her to go home and be the wife God wanted her to be. She talked with others in church, but no one would believe that Jason was capable of doing the things she claimed he did. Susan was beginning to get desperate.

Once after a particularly savage beating, she went to the police department in her small town. But Jason's brother was a police captain, and when he heard about the report of abuse he squelched it so the family name would not be smeared. He didn't believe Susan's "lies" either.

When Susan became pregnant with their first child, Jason refused to let her seek any medical attention. Susan felt like a prisoner. She was trapped. There was no place to go. No one would help her. She did slip away to see a Christian counselor a few times, but couldn't continue because she had no money.

After her second child was born, Jason's anger and rage became more frequent and more violent. He hadn't wanted a second child, and he said little Adam was Susan's fault. He would make her pay! One night in desperation Susan ran out into the night with nothing but the clothes on her back. She was so distraught for her own safety, she momentarily forgot about her two little children she left behind sound asleep. She ran to the home of neighbors who attended their church, but they would not take her in or do anything to help her. They told her to go back to her husband where she belonged.

But Jason would not let her come back; nor would he let her have the children. Susan's whole life crumbled to pieces; her dreams shattered. Eventually she was able to file for divorce, and she tried to win custody of her children. She got the divorce, but lost the children after Jason's brother, the police captain, testified in court that Susan had been to a "shrink" and that she was unstable and not fit to be a mother.

Now, five years after her disastrous, violent marriage to a man recommended by her pastor, Susan is trying to put the pieces of her life back together. She still does not have custody of her children and is only rarely permitted to even see them. Considering it all, she has so many questions. Why did the pastor encourage her to marry Jason? Why did she allow herself to be rushed into the marriage? Why did she stay in it so long? Why couldn't she see the signs of the problems that were to come? Why wasn't she alerted on her wedding night?

Susan is still searching for answers, but she is determined she will never allow herself to get into a situation like that again. She told Florence she is sure of one thing: "I will never again go to any man for counseling or guidance."

She doesn't feel any of us can be trusted. Could we blame her?

We thank Susan for sharing her story and for the insights she has shared with us about men who are abusive and the women who marry them. She is now working on her own book to try to help other women from making the same mistakes she made and to enable them to recognize the signs sooner than she did. She wants to spare other women the horrible experience she went through.

Why Do Some Men Abuse Their Wives?

Some men are abusing their wives and aren't even aware of it. Some know they're being abusive but have absolutely no idea why. What causes this kind of abusive personality?

I have never in forty-one years of marriage hit Florence, so I was never physically abusive. But I have already acknowledged that I had a critical and judgmental nature and that I often corrected her in front of other people. Perhaps I was not emotionally abusive, but I was surely emotionally overbearing and demanding. I'm not sure where one draws the line. Frankly, I never even had any sense of being critical, demanding, or overbearing. If someone had tried to tell me I was, I could have rationally and logically proved that I was not. If there were any problems, I could quickly summon up a list of the things and areas in which Florence fell short as a wife and a mate. This would clearly and correctly indicate where the real issues were: with Florence, naturally. Where else?

My own attitudes and logic were so typical of male thinking. It has taken a long time for me to see that I was filtering my views through cloudy lenses that prohibited me from discerning reality. Now, at last, I see clearly.

I would like to give you an opportunity to change your own lenses and take a new look at yourself. If there are some areas of your nature where you do not see yourself as others may see you, the following questions may help identify them for you.[1]

Assessing Your Potential for Aggression

Make a separate piece of paper your answer sheet; in a vertical column write the numbers one through thirty-eight. On this answer sheet simply write yes or no as your answer to each question corresponding to the various numbers. Indicate your total of yes answers for the various levels in the spaces provided here in the book. For the moment ignore the lines marked "Total W: ____." We'll get back to those later.

Level A

1. Would your wife say that you have tried to control her life by telling her who she can have for friends and who she cannot see?

2. Do you tend to be overly critical of your wife and frequently find fault with the way she does things?

3. Do you put her down in front of other people?

4. Have you had a tendency to call her names or tell her she's stupid or dumb—or make her feel that she is?

5. Does your wife have to be very careful to make sure she doesn't make you angry?

6. Is your wife afraid you might yell or swear at her?

Total of yes answers: ____   Total W: ____

Level B

7. Does your wife have to account to you for every dollar she spends?

8. Have you refused to allow your wife to have a credit card in her own name?

9. Do you make most of the financial decisions that affect the family without consulting your wife?

10. Have you ever refused to allow your wife to have any money because she disobeyed you?

11. Have you ever refused to give your wife money because she was not sexually willing?

12. Do you insist that your wife stay home and not work or have her own income, even when she wants to?

Total of yes answers: ____   Total W: ____

Level C

13. Have you refused to let your wife buy food or clothing for herself or the children?

14. Have you ever or would you be apt to buy a car or another big-ticket item for yourself when you have told your wife there was no money for household necessities for her or the children?

15. Have you ever yelled or cursed at your wife for buying something for herself or the children?

16. Have you ever bought things for your wife or used money to manipulate her so she would stay with you when she said she was going to leave?

Total of yes answers: _____   Total W: _____

Level D

17. Have you ever cursed or raged at your wife over things that were really pretty insignificant?

18. Do you often angrily accuse your wife of doing or saying something she insists she has not said or done and you later find she was telling the truth?

19. Do you have a tendency to lie to your wife or others to cover your own faults or mistakes?

20. Does your wife think or has she said that when you're with others or out in public you're a phony?

21. Have you ever publicly humiliated your wife?

22. Do you have a tendency to think or say that everybody else is stupid or that they don't know what they're talking about?

Total of yes answers: _____   Total W: _____

Level E

23. Have you ever put your fist through a wall, torn up a door, or destroyed furniture in your home?

24. Have you ever wrecked your kitchen, living room, bedroom, or other room in a fit of anger?

25. Have you ever thrown anything breakable or heavy at your wife?

26. Have you ever as an adult stolen, broken, or destroyed anything that did not belong to you?

27. Have you ever hit your wife or pushed her hard enough to make her fall down?

28. Have you ever cut off someone in your car or truck because the other driver did something that angered you?

29. Have you ever beaten or kicked a pet for no valid reason?

30. Have you ever been arrested or apprehended for fighting?

Total of yes answers: _____   Total W: _____

Level F

31. Have you ever threatened your wife, another family member, or a neighbor with a knife?

32. Have you ever hit your wife with anything other than your hand?

33. Have you ever physically abused your wife when she was pregnant?

34. Have your children or your wife ever had to stay home because of an injury you inflicted on them?

35. Has your wife ever tried to stop you from spanking or hitting one of your children because she was afraid you would physically harm the child?

36. Have you ever locked your wife (or your children without your wife's consent) in a room? Have you denied your wife the use of the telephone or car?

37. Has your wife ever had to call the police because of your violence?

38. Have you ever threatened to kill your wife or any of your children?

Total of yes answers:_____   Total W:_____

Grand total of yes answers _____   **Grand Total W:**_____

The questions you responded to and the number of yes answers you gave will give you a fairly clear idea of how you perceive yourself. Your answers will also help you assess your potential for aggression. Each additional level of questions indicates a growing propensity toward domestic violence. If you only answered yes in the first two levels your issues are clear but less severe. The more yes answers you gave in the succeeding levels the more severe your problem and the more urgent it is for you to face the turbulence that is probably raging within your soul. Wake up before you have more serious consequences to face!

There is one more step you should take to assure that you are perceiving yourself accurately. We all tend to see ourselves through our own eyes, that is, *subjectively* rather than *objectively*, as others see us. Much of the time we are completely unaware of things that are very clear to others, especially our family and our co-workers. I remember a number of years ago coming into my office and finding a brief note on my desk from one of the women in our office. She had quit with no notice because, she said, "I can't stand to live with your anger any longer." I was shocked. I never thought I had gotten angry in the office, but I did remember having to be patient with this woman for what I thought were excessive oversights. I didn't see myself as she saw me.

Are you prepared to grant someone else the right to answer these same questions about you "objectively"? The first person you should think about asking is your wife.

Asking Your Wife for Input

Ask your wife to make an answer sheet with a vertical column numbered from one to thirty-eight, then ask her to answer each question about you to the best of her knowledge. Ask her to enter the number of her yes answers in each level on the line marked "Total W: _____ " on the appropriate page of the book where that level of questions appears.

While your wife is answering the questions, leave the room so she can answer truthfully without any fear that you might question her answers. There will be time for that later. There is no purpose in her answering the questions if she thinks she can only answer them the way you want her to. When she is finished, go through the questions together, comparing your respective totals of yes answers for each level. On those levels where they are the same or close, perhaps a difference of only one, you can feel confident that you both see you about the same way. If there is a significant difference: **Caution!** . . . **Go slowly!**

When these differences occur, immediately move into your listening mode. Switch into spiritual communication, surrendering yourself and your emotions to the Lord and asking Him to take immediate control of your life. Ask Him to help you control any anger that might flare up! This becomes increasingly important if your wife has answered yes to several questions in levels C and D to which you did not respond. *If she answered yes to several of the questions in levels E or F, you should probably not attempt to review these questions without the presence of a mutually agreeable third person, preferably a man you both respect.* It is possible that your reactions to some of her yes answers and explanations of them could become violent or abusive. Protect yourself and your family. *Have a third person there with you.*

Understanding the Assessment Levels

Each of the six levels of the assessment represents your increasing propensity toward domestic violence or your past history of emotional or family-control issues that have led to violence. The most important answers may not be yours but your wife's. Her answers will alert you to problem areas of your life that you may be totally unaware of that are robbing your family of the best you would want for them.

Level A indicates troubling but probably not dangerous levels of emotional control over your wife and family. The lack of freedom and responsibility you are allowing your family members causes them to fear you and makes it very difficult for them to love you, trust you, and respect you. While your wife may be strong enough to survive this kind of control, it would not be surprising if your children became rebellious disappointments in their teenage or later years. Do something now about yourself before it's too late. The reasons you feel the need to exercise this kind of control over your family may be due to repressed anger and/or low self-worth in you. Where did those feelings come from? Reading some of the books we have already mentioned, talking with your wife, and talking with your pastor or a Christian counselor could help you greatly.

Level B shows you have an unhealthy need to control your wife financially. You should understand that your wife not only has a right to understand family finances, she also must have funds she can spend totally at her own discretion, whether this money comes from your own earnings or from hers. She must have the right to control certain areas of her own life without interference from you. If she had several yes answers in this level, release her; don't treat her like a dummy. Sit down together and come to some agreements about (1) Those areas in which she will take full responsibility, (2) Those areas in which you will *mutually agree*, including all areas affecting family financial welfare, such as major purchases, and (3) Those areas for which you take full responsibility, including your own personal expenditures for your daily necessities.

Level C shows a pronounced self-focus. Yes answers to these questions would indicate you have been more concerned with your own needs than with those of your family. This may have created a severely unhealthy family atmosphere, probably due to some deeply entrenched rejection or deprivation issues within you. The real roots of these problems may be serious, complex issues that are crying out to be acknowledged and corrected.

Level D addresses serious levels of emotional abuse of your wife and family. Lying and humiliating your wife are not minor issues to be glossed over. Within you there may be raging waves of repressed anger. The source of such anger is usually severe and traumatic childhood abuse and victimization. Take steps now to deal with these feelings that even you probably don't understand. Our books *Freeing Your Mind from Memories That Bind* and *The Promise of Healing* could be useful as a starting point in helping you find resolution and restoration. Counseling for this level of hurts may be essential to help you understand what is truly happening and what your life can be like when these issues are properly addressed and brought to the Lord for cleansing and healing.

Level E shows you are already capable of significant physical violence. Further anger and abuse by you may cause serious grief for both you and for your family. Do not treat this lightly or as something that will soon pass away! It rarely does. It usually gets worse. Do not fool yourself into thinking this is normal behavior or that your wife should just get used to it or, even worse, that she deserves it. Any such thoughts simply indicate a sense of denial and your unwillingness to face your problems. Take action to help yourself now, before it is too late. Effective Christian counseling may be essential for you to see what is going on inside yourself.

Level F means FAMILY BEWARE! Yes answers to these questions are symptoms of potentially life-threatening physical violence. Immediate outside intervention is probably needed to protect you from doing even further serious harm to your family and yourself. This is the most extreme and perilous level of abusive action. If both you and your wife were abused during childhood, your wife most likely has her own serious anger problems due to the abuse she also suffered. Her eruptions of anger may be triggering your own volcano of rage that explodes wildly out of control. If you or your wife have answered yes to these questions, we urge you to commit before the Lord to do everything you can to find the root of your volatile nature and to deal with it. *Get help now!* Resolve with your wife *today* that you will seek answers and solutions to return you both to the emotional health and stability God wants for you. It is going to take effort, but you will never regret it.

As you have reviewed your own and your wife's responses to these questions, what have you learned about yourself? Does your wife have an abusive husband? And if she does is there hope for you? The answer is *yes!* There is hope for you and for all those who bring their struggles to the Lord Jesus.

Seeing above Life's Weeds

Hundreds, probably thousands, of men have changed from being violent, abusive husbands and fathers to being the kind of loving, Christian men God wants as leaders of families. One of those men was Russ Parker. If there is hope for Russ, there is hope for you. Here is his story, which he has shared with us in the hope that others might profit from his experiences.

My most significant struggle in my marriage to Cindy has been dealing with my anger. It wasn't that I was easily irritated or upset, but that I lashed out with very deep-seated anger, rage, and violence—physical abuse. From the beginning of our marriage nearly thirty years ago, I allowed my temper and tongue to rule me. I threw things at Cindy. I destroyed precious keepsakes in our home. I threatened her. I physically abused her. I was unaware of why I had such anger or where it came from; it was too deeply buried inside me.

When things grew progressively worse I sought help from pastors, marriage counselors, psychologists, and psychiatrists. Throughout all of this counseling there was never any attempt to learn where my anger came from, only what triggered it. I learned to put a band-aid on the problem or, more realistically, a lid on the pressure cooker. That caused me to hold in my anger, letting it build up until I exploded in rage and violence.

Cindy and I went through several separations. I kept making promises that I wouldn't abuse her again, and each time I really believed I could keep my word to her. I tried to deal with my anger and rage on my own, but despite my best and sincere intentions, my attempts always failed.

When Cindy left me the last time and I had no idea of where she was, I had no one to turn to but Jesus. He raised the shade of denial enough so I could see my pitiful condition and my need for help. I began participating in Bible studies and sought professional help again, working hard to overcome my anger and control my temper. After six months Cindy came back and we tried again. I managed to maintain partial control over my anger, but that maintenance was based on my fear of losing Cindy, not on my healing. I *wasn't* healed.

The beginning of real change came when Cindy and I attended one of the Littauers' CLASS seminars. I will never forget when Florence described the need to be clean on the inside. She told us we needed to get rid of our emotional garbage and let God haul it away. Then Fred shared some of the struggles he had faced in his life and the changes that had begun when he started writing his prayers every day.

After meeting with Fred personally, I saw the need to look into my past. I realized there was a reason for all the anger bottled up inside me, and I needed to find out what it was. I needed cleansing and healing. It was time to let Jesus work within me. At Fred's suggestion I began writing my prayers each day, and as a result I started experiencing a relationship with the Lord Jesus I had never imagined possible.

A few months later I attended my first Promise of Healing Workshop, another major step forward. It confirmed what Fred had shared with me at the CLASS seminar, that my anger was the direct result of my having been abused physically, emotionally, and sexually as a child.

As the months progressed, my prayer life improved as each day I wrote to the Lord. God continued to do His healing work in me, and I learned to understand, accept, and trust Him. He began showing me many forgotten memories from my childhood. But I still struggled with one concern, the possibility that I had been sexually abused when I was little. I was fervently asking the Lord to reveal anything He wanted me to know from my childhood. What had happened to me? Who had done it?

Cindy and I decided to attend a second Promise Workshop. On the second morning Fred invited us all to listen for the Lord's voice as we wrote our prayers. I had never known I could actually hear His voice, but as I wrote in my prayer journal that morning, here is what I wrote to Jesus and here are His answers to me:

"Dear Jesus."

"Yes, My child."

"I love You."

"I know."

"Jesus, I love You. I have asked for help from You so often I think I know how You will answer me."

"You look away from Me."

"I guess I do . . . I don't mean to or want to."

"Russ, take My hands and hold on. I want to lift you high above the weeds so you can see clearly."

"What do You want to show me?"

"Your childhood hurts."

"Jesus, I'm afraid."

"Trust Me, Russ, and realize that I love you, My little one. Wake up, and you will realize that I am all you will ever need. I want you to know I will always be with you."

So I said, "OK, Lord, I'm ready. Reveal the truth to me, the truth that would set me free." Then I saw clearly the sexual violation that was done to me when I was only four years old. It had been buried in the deepest recesses of my mind. Now I understood where all my anger came from. It was as if a huge weight had been lifted from my shoulders. Jesus had already shown me several "weed patches" in my childhood. Now He lifted me up so I could see *above* the weeds. He continues to remove the weeds of my past.

Only Jesus can reveal and heal. No psychiatrist can do this. God must clean us on the inside and make us new. Jesus is creating a clean heart and mind inside me, and He is renewing His Spirit within me. My anger is decreasing daily, and my healing journey is continuing. I am so thankful for the changes He is making in my life and in my relationship with Cindy. She is even learning she can trust me!

If you are recognizing now that you have been an abusive husband to your wife, why not follow Russ's example? Get to the roots. Dig up the weeds. Let the Lord Jesus set you free!

13

HOW CAN THE HUSBAND BE THE HEAD OF THE WIFE?

You may have already gathered that in my own Christian life I have two passions. The first is the essential importance of daily prayer. The second is the awesome power of the Lord to bring miraculous healing and transformation into the dark places of our lives. But there is another Christian principle I cherish, although I rarely feel at liberty to share my understanding of it because of its tendency to cause controversy. What is this Christian principle I love but do not often discuss? It is the scriptural-defined relationship and roles of the husband and wife.

Florence and I know full well that Christians are split on their understanding of doctrines and teachings. We try to carefully avoid these topics in our workshops and seminars because we work in churches of several different denominations around the world and we rarely know the individual church's or pastor's position on the specific issues. We try to be very careful never to present anything that might be controversial or cause an unintended offense, so I have steered clear of discussing my understanding of the husband's scriptural role as head of the wife.

But a book is different. Within these pages I feel the freedom to share with you what I strongly believe Scripture teaches about headship, about

authority, and about submission. I have studied all the correlative passages of Scripture about this issue that I could find, and I have sought
the mind of God. He has answered me with the feeling of peace that tells
me I have understood His will and intent. I have applied these truths,
as I believe the Lord has revealed them, to my own relationship with
Florence. And I have seen amazing changes in how she responds to me
when my life, my words, and my deeds are consistent with what God
teaches us.

Why such a long introduction to this topic? Because the ideas I am
going to present to you may be somewhat different from what you have
been taught or heard in the past. These concepts are not radical, unusual,
or unsupported by others who have searched the Scriptures trying to
understand the mind of God. Many others see this question the same way
I do. But much of the public teaching and the perceptions that people
receive from it are apt to be quite different. I believe these misperceptions
lead to a subtle but surprisingly significant bondage for both husbands and
wives. I offer you this "new" perspective on headship and authority in the
home, so that you, too, might search the Scriptures and seek the mind
of God for yourself. Then, as Gamaliel, a respected doctor of the Jewish
law, stated, "If this counsel be of men, it will come to nought: But if it
be of God, ye cannot overthrow it; lest haply ye be found even to fight
against God" (Acts 5:38–39).

It is not our Redeemer's intent or desire for us to remain in any form
of bondage or captivity. David cried out unto the Lord, "Bring my soul
out of prison, that I may praise thy name" (Ps. 142:7). In Isaiah 61:1, God
told us in advance of His mission, and in Luke 4:18 Jesus repeated it:
"The Spirit of the Lord is upon me, because he hath anointed me
to . . . preach deliverance to the captives, and . . . to set at liberty
them that are bruised."

Many men have been bound and bruised by trying to be something God
never intended us to be. We thought we had all the answers, that we must
make all the decisions, that we were the authority in the home, that only
we men received the word directly from the Lord, and that therefore our
wives must obey us. As a result our wives have been battered and brushed
aside, and we have taken on the lonely responsibility for our families without the benefit of our wives' insight, wisdom, and guidance. Now we must
wake up and know the mind of the Lord. Hearing someone else's understanding of the Lord's Word is not sufficient. We must diligently search
the Scriptures ourselves to know the truth. Then we must test the spirits
to see whether they are of God. Finally we must ask in prayer for the peace
that passes understanding so we may know we are in fact hearing the mind

of the Lord as He intended. "A threefold cord is not quickly broken" (Eccles. 4:12).

If Not the Husband, Who Is the Authority?

What does this mean? Doesn't the husband have authority in his own home? Isn't that what Scripture teaches? The answer must be no! Why? Because the Lord Jesus Christ is to be the only authority in the home! "*All authority* has been given to Me in heaven and on earth" (Matt. 28:18 NASB). The Lord, Himself, has *all* authority in heaven, on earth, in the church, and obviously in the homes of believers. The husband is not the authority, for then there would be *two authorities* in the home. And as Matthew 6:24 tells us, "No one can serve two masters; for either he [or she] will hate the one and love the other, or he [or she] will hold to one and despise the other" (NASB). James 1:8 reinforces this principle, stating, "A double minded man is unstable in all his ways."

While this understanding of God's will seems obvious to many Christians, it is not easy for some to accept this interpretation. This was demonstrated not long ago when Florence was the main speaker for a large women's retreat in Colorado and, in an exception to our no-controversy rule, I shared my understanding of the husband's headship and authority when I was invited to teach an afternoon workshop on the roles of the husband and wife.

I shared what I believed the Scripture clearly teaches: that only the Lord can be the authority in the home, and that the husband and wife, being one in the scriptural and spiritual sense, must be submitted to one another. Both must be submitted and surrendered to the Lord. I presented all the scriptural verification of this perspective that time permitted, and almost all of the forty or so women in the session were expressively enthusiastic. Many came up afterward and told me how freeing this perspective made them feel. They also said they thought it would make their husbands feel free as well because the men wouldn't have to carry the weight of all family decisions and authority alone. The women realized family responsibilities need to be shared, and they accepted my interpretation that Scripture teaches this principle. They said they couldn't wait to get home to share this new perspective with their husbands.

While this was true for most of the women in the workshop, it was not true for all of them, especially for two who waited after the others left to express their angry reactions. After the other participants' enthusiastic support, their anger caught me somewhat off guard. They believed strongly that only the husband was the authority in the home, that he must make all decisions and the wife must simply obey whatever he decides. Another woman, standing nearby and overhearing their criticism, told me after they left, "Don't let them get you down. They're using that as a crutch so they don't have to take responsibility for anything. You pushed them out of their comfort zone."

Looking for Answers

While many wives are comfortable letting their husbands carry total responsibility for their families, many men are likewise comfortable in having total authority. After all, it's surely easier to make decisions alone than to consider someone else's viewpoint and carefully weigh all the pros and cons. But I am convinced that Scripture teaches otherwise. Why? Come along and I'll lead you through the scriptural journey that revealed the answers to me.

Let's begin at the beginning, in Genesis: "Therefore shall a man leave his father and his mother, and shall cleave unto his wife: and the two shall become one flesh" (2:24). This truth is such an important part of Scripture that it is repeated no fewer than five times, once in the Old Testament and four times in the New (Gen. 2:24, Matt. 19:5–6, Mark 10:7–8, 1 Cor. 6:16, and Eph. 5:31). I am not aware of any other single passage that is repeated more than this one. In addition, there are at least two other passages that directly relate to this concept of the two becoming one (see John 17:22 and Gal. 3:28).

What happens when two of anything become one? What happens when two companies merge and become one corporation? What happened when thirteen colonies became one nation? What happens when a husband and wife join their two bodies? They become ONE. And remember that Jesus said, "I and my Father are one" (John 10:30; see also John 10:38 and 17:22). Think of two round circles of paint, one blue and one yellow, on a piece of wax paper. As you lift the sides of the wax paper the two circles run *into* each other. How many circles are there now? Just one? And what color is the circle? It's green! The two have become one. The individual properties of the two paints are still present, but they have become one new paint.

Two become one. This is God's order for the husband-wife relationship. This is unity: the one mind, one body, one heart, one soul that the Bible speaks about.

Now think about this: When two equal parts merge together, which one is dominant? What is your answer? When the thirteen colonies merged, which one was in charge? When two similar circles of paint merge into one, which one is dominant? When a husband and wife merge their lives in the sight of God, which one is in charge? The answer in each case must be the same: No one entity, or person, is in charge. The separate parts become equally subject to a higher authority.

Let's look at this question from another perspective. Are these two parts, husband and wife, the same? No. Men and women have bodies that differ, emotions that differ, and in the family, a nuclear part of the body of Christ, they have *functions* that differ. These functions are a most important part of understanding this whole question. We will discuss this facet of the scriptural concept in a moment. But first let's look at another question: Are the husband and wife *equal* in the sight of God? Again we must turn to Scripture:

> So God created man [that is, mankind] in his own image, in the image of God created he him; male and female created he them. (Gen. 1:27)

> From the beginning of creation, God made them male and female. (Mark 10:6; see also Matt. 19:4 NASB)

> In the Lord, neither is woman independent of man, nor is man independent of woman. For as the woman originates from the man, so also the man has his birth through the woman; and all things originate from God. (1 Cor. 11:11–12 NASB)

> The wife does not have authority over her own body, but the husband does; and likewise also the husband does not have authority over his own body, but the wife does. (1 Cor. 7:4 NASB)

> There is neither Jew nor Greek, there is neither bond nor free, there is neither male nor female: for *ye are all one in Christ Jesus*. (Gal. 3:28)

> You husbands . . . *grant her honor* as a fellow heir of the grace of life, so that your prayers may not be hindered. (1 Pet. 3:7 NASB)

What does it mean to be a fellow heir? The Greek word used here is *sugkleronomos*, which describes "one who participates in the same lot. . . . [Referring] to a *personal equality* based on an equality of possession."[1] Can one equal have authority over another equal? The answer must be no; otherwise they would no longer be equals. Scripture clearly shows us that man and woman, male and female, husband and wife *are equal*. But if they are equal what does Ephesians 5:23 mean when it clearly states "the husband is the head of the wife"?

To understand any biblical principle we must search the whole body of Scripture to see that there is harmony. "God is not the author of confusion, but of peace" (1 Cor. 14:33). His wisdom is "first pure, then peaceable, gentle, and easy to be intreated [persuaded], full of mercy and good fruits" (James 3:17). We must be careful that we do not base a position on a single verse if it is not consistent with the whole body of truth, the whole counsel of God. This is how misconstructions are most apt to occur.

That the husband is the head of the wife is without question. Scripture makes this a certainty. The position that he is the authority *over* the wife, however, is not consistent with the body of Scripture we have examined. Therefore, if the husband is not the authority over the wife, if he is not her *lord*, then saying that she must obey him, that he has the right of lordship over her, is inconsistent and must be deemed faulty. Proponents of this faulty position generally refer to Titus 2:5, which advises older women to teach younger women "to be discreet, chaste, keepers at home, good, obedient to their own husbands." The use of the word *obedient* in the King James Version is generally considered to be an inferior rendering. Virtually all scholarly translations prefer instead the translation *being subject*. Also, because this passage speaks of the older women's responsibility to teach the younger women, it therefore portrays what is to be the *wife's* condition, *not the husband's* position. This is an important differentiation.

Another facet of this principle, that the wife must be subject to her husband, that she must be submitted to him, is also not subject to question. This is clearly stated in Ephesians 5:22 and affirmed in Colossians 3:18 and 1 Peter 3:1.

Who Does God Instruct First?

When you look at these three passages of Scripture related to wives being subject to their husbands you may notice an interesting and curious side note. In each case this instruction is given first to wives, then to husbands! Why this consistency? Is there a significance? Scripture itself does not answer these questions. We can only ponder this certainty and draw our own conclusions, realizing that nothing is in Scripture by chance. Every word, every "jot and tittle" is by design and is placed, in the original manuscripts, exactly as God intended.

Why do you think God chose to instruct wives first and then to give His instruction to husbands? I have thought about this question many times and posed it to both men and women. One answer I have heard (and one that I tend to agree with), is that God knows the differing natures of men and women, and He knows women tend to be more readily responsive, more in tune, to matters of the Spirit than men do. When a husband and wife are struggling and the idea to go to someone for help or counseling comes up, who initiates it? Counselors and pastors will consistently tell you it's invariably the wife! And who do you think is usually the first one to quit, saying something like, "I don't need this." Invariably, it's the husband! When a husband and wife go to someone for help, the husband's attitude is often *There's nothing the matter with me. If she would only shape up and be what I want her to be, we wouldn't have any problems!* Be honest. Does this sound familiar to you?

Men, what's wrong with us? We're just as interested as our wives in having peace and harmony in our homes, aren't we? Then why do so many of us allow our wives to take the first step toward achieving it? Are you starting to understand why God gave His instructions about the marriage relationship to women first?

Perhaps another reason He addresses women first is that we men tend to have a pride barrier. As a rule we are very reluctant to discuss with anyone those issues that get too close to our emotions and feelings. We rarely are able to discuss these things with the person who is closest to us, the person who should be our best friend: our wife. Men seldom discuss their deep feelings with each other.

This was demonstrated for me many years ago. I had been visiting a new church and on about the fourth Sunday I'd been there an acquaintance invited me to visit his men's Bible study class after the service. I had been enjoying the church service, the music, and the preaching, so I accepted with joy. We went to a small room where six or seven other men joined us. After several minutes of relatively inane banter and introductions they began a seemingly inconsequential discussion of the weekly lesson. All of this had been very pleasant, though not personally penetrating. Then came the time for prayer and requests. I was stunned that this group of men who had been meeting together for months knew almost nothing about each other. The few prayer requests appeared to be very impersonal and remote from what must have been going on in their lives. I wondered to myself *Don't these men have any problems at all? Am I the only one who is struggling with any issues in my life?* Needless to say, even though I continued to worship at that church when I was in town, I felt no sense of being drawn to return to the men's class.

It was not until several years later, when I found myself ministering to the man (who had invited me to the class) and his wife, that I learned of the very severe and deep issues in both their lives. They were struggling with problems they had had when I attended that class, and they are still working through them today. But no one would have guessed that he or any of the others had any problems that Sunday morning. So many of us men put on our plastic smiles and head for church on Sunday morning, giving every evidence that we have life fully under control. Because most of us tend to wear this unreal facade, anyone would be reluctant to share his hurts lest he be considered unmanly or unusual. Our pride barrier keeps us from opening up and sharing our deepest needs and feelings.

But our Father in heaven knows each of us well. He knows we men are often slow to respond to Him. He knows we are hesitant to seek help, that we find it easier to focus on our wives as the imperfect one, the one who needs help, the one who needs to change. He knows about this pride issue. And I think He knows our wives are more apt to set the tone for healthy change in the home. *I think He knows that in reality most of our wives are actually the spiritual leaders in our homes, and in many respects our wives are actually the heads of our homes!* It ought not to be so. I think that is why He gave the instructions in all three places to wives first.

What Does Submission Mean?

We have already seen that God created a man and his wife to be one flesh, and we have seen that He created them as spiritual equals. We have also seen that Jesus can be the only authority in the home. And we've identified the scriptures in which God tells wives first, and then their husbands, that the wife is to be submitted, or subject, to her husband. Now let's look at what this submission really means.

The answer lies clearly and simply in an often-overlooked verse in Ephesians: "Submitting yourselves one to another in the fear [reverence] of God" (5:21). When studying this verse it helps if we read this entire passage, verses 21–28, clearly tying in verse 21 to the whole text. It describes how and why the wife must submit to her husband (vv. 22–24) and how the husband must treat and regard his wife (vv. 25 and 28). When we do, we read this instruction:

> Submitting yourselves [voluntarily] one to another in the fear
> of God. Wives, submit yourselves unto your husbands. . . .
> Husbands, love your wives, even as Christ also loved the
> church, and gave himself for it.

When we husbands understand that we are to love our wives the same way Christ loved the church, we get a clearer understanding of what that kind of love means in the relationship. Christ gave Himself for the church. He voluntarily surrendered His will in obedience to God. He submitted Himself, His very life. "So ought men to love their wives" (v. 28). Our Lord Jesus demonstrated to us the nature of what our love for our wives should be. It is to be *giving*, and to give also means to submit, to surrender our will. This is completely in harmony with verse 21 in which both husbands and wives are directed to submit to each other.

Who, then, is to submit? What is the answer to the submission question? Scripture clearly teaches us that I am to be submitted to Florence and she to me. Likewise you are to be completely submitted to your wife and she to you.

One of the best definitions I have ever seen of the word *submission* is "voluntary selflessness." This means I always endeavor to put my wife's needs, desires, and wishes ahead of my own. It also means that I try at all times to treat her like a queen, like a beautiful, precious, fragile flower. How do you think Florence feels when she knows I am always putting her interests ahead of my own, that I am always doing my very best to take care of her, nurture her, provide for her, and protect her? How do you think she reacts when she knows that, aside of my love for the Lord, my love for her is always preeminent in my mind and motivation? Frankly, a woman finds it hard to resist a man who treats her that way!

Of course, I would like it very much if she were to understand Scripture the very same way and treat me as that handsome hunk of a man she adores and respects, looks up to and trusts, and brags about to her friends. I would like it if she always tried to put a priority on my needs and desires. Isn't that what "voluntary selflessness" means? Isn't that what submission means? Can you imagine how life would be if we both made that our goal and each of us diligently strived to make that a reality in our marriage? Now, finally, in our forty-first year of marriage, this is exactly the way we relate to each other. Florence knows I am completely submitted to her, that I am voluntarily selfless, and she is also fully submitted to me and my needs and desires. We have put God's instructions into practice and it should not be a surprise to anybody that it works! God's laws always do.

God's law of mutual submission will work in your home, too. I am reminded of John 13:17, "Now that you know this truth, how happy you will be if you put it into practice!" (TEV). I am happy, and I am fulfilled as a man and a husband. My only regret is that I didn't know and understand this principle years earlier. Had I been aware of its significance we might have enjoyed our current marriage relationship many years sooner. But back then I had a lot of emotional trash and baggage to get rid of before I could earn my wife's love and respect. We had some rebuilding that had to be done before she felt she could trust her emotions to me, before her fear of my anger was gone. We husbands can never *command* respect. It's like that clever investment-company's commercial that insists they make money the old-fashioned way: We have to *earn it!*

One word of caution: This instruction for mutual submission is not *conditional*. It does not mean you are only to do it for your wife if she does it for you. Jesus' examples to us were never conditional. He always did those things that were pleasing to His Father in heaven, no matter how others responded. Do you want to be the leader of your household? Do you want to be the head of your wife? Then by definition you must take the initiative and put this truth into practice. Let her see that you are a Christian husband who is worthy of her respect and her trust; then she will want to follow you.

So What Exactly Does Headship Mean?

We have seen that *headship* cannot mean *lordship* because the husband is not and cannot be the authority over the wife. We have also seen that the popular chain-of-command interpretation cannot be valid because the wife is not under the husband's authority; she is spiritually equal. Yet Ephesians 5:23 clearly states that "the husband is the head of the wife, even as Christ is the head of the church," and 1 Corinthians 11:3 says, "The head of every man is Christ; and the head of the woman is the man; and the head of Christ is God."

Let us begin this study by trying to understand the significance of God as the head of Christ. Does this mean God has authority over Christ? We already understand that the Father, the Son, and the Holy Spirit are one. These are the three parts of the one Godhead. The Lord Himself clearly states "that they all may be one; as thou, Father, art in me, and I in thee, . . . that they may be one, even as we are one" (John 17:21–22). And in John 10:30 and 38 He states, "I and my Father are one. . . . The Father is in me, and I in him."

Are you struggling with this concept? Philip, one of Jesus' own disciples, also had difficulty understanding it. "Jesus said to him, 'Have I been so long with you, and yet you have not come to know Me, Philip? He who has seen Me has seen the Father; how do you say, 'Show us the Father'? Do you not believe that I am in the Father, and the Father is in Me? . . . Believe Me, that I am in the Father, and the Father in Me" (John 14:9–11 NASB).

One of my most interesting studies in understanding this scriptural principle was in searching out all the different functions I could find for the three parts of the Godhead: the Father, Son, and Holy Spirit. I became interested in this study from 1 Corinthians 12:4–6, which states:

> Now there are varieties of gifts, but the same Spirit. And there are varieties of ministries, and the same Lord. And there are varieties of effects, but the same God. (NASB)

These verses showed me that each part of the Godhead had clearly defined and distinct functions. The Holy Spirit gives the gifts. The Lord gives the ministries where the gifts are to be exercised, and the Father determines the effects of the gifts. It was interesting to me that as I searched through both the Old and New Testaments I found no duplication in the functions of the Trinity, save one. Both the Son and the Spirit are our intercessors before the Father! In their perfect oneness the three parts of the Godhead have specific roles in the kingdom of heaven; yet in their unique oneness they function in perfect harmony without overlapping or question of authority. So it is to be in the relationship between husband and wife.

The Scriptures frequently use figures of speech to illustrate a truth just as the Lord used many parables to teach the disciples. The word *head* is one of these figures of speech, also known as a *metaphor* (a word or phrase used in place of another to suggest a likeness between them). Realizing this, suddenly the meaning of that word *headship* became clear for me. It is a *function of responsibility* rather than a *position of authority*, as it is often described. "For just as we have many members in one body and all the members do not have the same function, so we, who are many, are one body in Christ, and individually members one of another" (Rom. 12:4–5 NASB).

When we read that "the husband is the *head* of the wife" we need to understand that *head* is used as a metaphor, a figure of speech, to suggest the relationship of the husband with the rest of the body. We can readily see that the husband is an integral part of the body; he is the head, the top, the summit, the leader. But nowhere is it unequivocally stated that he is the ruler or the authority! Even in the analogy used in Scripture the head is not the ruler of the body. All parts of the body are placed in the body just as God wills and each has its own purpose or function, as described clearly in the verses that follow:

> For the body is not one member, but many. If the foot should say, "Because I am not a hand, I am not a part of the body," it is not for this reason any the less a part of the body. And if

the ear should say, "Because I am not an eye, I am not a part
of the body," it is not for this reason any the less a part of the
body. If the whole body were an eye, where would the hearing be? If the whole were hearing, where would the sense of
smell be? But now God has placed the members, each one of
them, in the body, just as He desired. . . . that there should
be no division in the body, but that the members should have
the same care for one another. (1 Cor 12:14–18, 25 NASB)

The husband and the wife then are equally important members of the
body, but they have functions that differ. They are not the same, but they
are equal. They exist in harmony, working out the purposes or functions
God has ascribed to them. With this as our understanding we see that
all truths of Scripture are in harmony and in agreement.

Now we can understand the verse that says, "The wife does not have
authority over her own body, but the husband does; and likewise also the
husband does not have authority over his own body, but the wife does"
(1 Cor. 7:4 NASB).

Can there be any question now about who is the authority in the home?
It must always be the Lord Jesus Christ and none other. The husband and
wife must function as equal parts of their unity. Neither should try to exercise power or authority over the other. Anything else is in contradis-
tinction to the will of God as given in Scripture and precludes the full
blessings God would bestow on the family. Yes, the husband is to be the
spiritual leader, the head of the wife; that is his function. But is he to be
the authority? No, God has not given him that position.

If you or your wife have subscribed to the interpretation that the
husband is the *authority* over the wife and therefore she must *blindly obey
him*, I would urge you not to simply accept what I have presented here.
Instead I strongly encourage you to do your own study and research on
this subject, reviewing the verses that have been used in this chapter.
Several good Greek word-study dictionaries are available to assist you in
understanding and grasping the mind of God on this very important
question. As you do your study, pray and ask the Lord to reveal truth to
you. Ask Him to inscribe on your heart His purpose for you and your
home. If you ask He will answer, and the Holy Spirit will "guide you into
all truth" (John 16:13). And when you know the truth, "the truth shall
make you free" (John 8:32). You will no longer be in bondage, thinking
you must make all the decisions in your family alone, without the benefit of your wife's insight, counsel, and guidance.

We penalize ourselves when we don't avail ourselves of our wives'
wisdom. "Where no counsel is, the people fall: but in the multitude of

counselors there is safety. . . . The way of a fool is right in his own eyes: but he that hearkeneth unto counsel is wise" (Prov. 11:14 and 12:15). How much grief I could have spared myself in the past if I had listened to my wife's counsel or heeded her concerns! Now, at last, I have learned.

Including Our Wives in Family Decision-Making

God created our wives to be our helpers, to be an important part of our team. He gave them understanding and perception that we husbands often don't have. They can see things we don't see. Therefore they need to be a part of the decision-making process about everything that affects the family.

Obviously there are certain minor decisions about things that affect no one else that we can make ourselves. (I am presuming for these relatively minor decisions that you are already seeking the mind of Christ through daily prayer with Him and that He is, therefore, directing your path.) For example, I do not ask my wife what I should wear each day. That decision I make myself. On the other hand, if we are going someplace special and I know my appearance will be important to her, I might ask her what she would like me to wear. Sometimes she likes our outfits to coordinate. Is this infringing upon my freedom? No, I don't feel it is because my ultimate desire is to please my wife in every way I can! I am simply putting her needs and desires ahead of my own. "Do nothing from selfishness . . . but let each of you regard the other as more important than yourself" (paraphrase of Phil. 2:3 NASB). Likewise, my wife makes those decisions that only affect her. I do not question her about these decisions, and I do not help her unless she asks. And I am the leader in doing this. By my actions, not by my words, I set the tone in our relationship for mutual submission, voluntary selflessness. Like an officer in battle I am leading the charge, not telling the troops to go on ahead of me. My wife finds it both easy and comfortable to follow this kind of leadership.

How do we make the major decisions, those that affect us jointly or affect our family as a whole? We look first to God for our answers. The Scriptures speak again and again about the importance of unity among the body. The family, being a micro-unit of the body of Christ, falls within this framework. "Now I beseech you, brethren, by the name of our Lord Jesus Christ, that ye all speak the same thing, and that there be no divisions among you; but that ye be perfectly joined together in the same mind and in the same judgment" (1 Cor. 1:10). "Be of one mind, live in peace; and the God of love and peace shall be with you" (2 Cor. 13:11). "For He is our peace, who hath made both one, and hath broken down the middle wall of partition between us" (Eph. 2:14). "Finally, *be ye all of one mind,* having compassion one of another" (1 Pet. 3:8).

These are only a few of the many verses that enjoin oneness and accord, and they apply to the husband and wife as well as to all Christians. They show us how God expects us to make our decisions: We are to be likeminded, in agreement.

First, we analyze together all aspects of the issue we are considering. Second, we count the costs so we can ascertain, to the best of our ability, that we can complete the project and that it will not cause undue stress or strain upon us. Third, together we weigh all the factors involved in reaching our decision to see if we are in agreement. If we are of one mind, we can proceed. If we are not in accord, we pause until we do have unity of mind. If we do not, we simply shelve or discard the question. It is far better to make no decision than to make one that is going to cause grief or pain later.

If you are considering a decision that involves a substantial commitment, such as a major purchase, private school for the children, a job change that would mean uprooting the family, or anything that might make a significant impact upon the family or one of its members, there is an important fourth step: PRAY! Ask the Lord either to confirm your decision or to remove the peace, or the accord, you initially had about it if it is not His will for you. If you ask Him, He will do it.

There is an important value in decisions made in accord with one another. If, in the light of experience, we see that we made a poor decision, we both hold ourselves equally accountable. There is no finger pointing. There is no "I told you so" and no second-guessing of the other. We made the decision together. We agreed on it, and now we will rise or fall together on whatever the outcome may be. It does not affect our respect or our trust of one another. We made the decision in unison, we were in complete agreement, and we remain harmoniously bound to each other! If there are lessons for us to learn we learn together. "Two are better than one; because they have a good reward for their labour. For if they fall, the one will lift up his fellow: but woe to him that is alone when he falleth; for he hath not another to help him up" (Eccles. 4:9–10).

A Word about the Functions of Husbands

We have already discussed how the statement that the husband is the head of the wife refers scripturally to a function of responsibility rather than to a position of authority. Briefly, let us see how Scripture portrays some of those functions of the husband:

Protector. Christ provided all the spiritual weapons we need to protect ourselves, the church, and our families against the spiritual attacks of the enemy (Eph. 6:10–18). We are to be the spiritual leader, the head. We should also be first in scriptural knowledge, understanding, and wisdom. One of the tragedies of modern life is that in many homes the wife is spiritually far ahead of the husband. On average, women spend far more time in Bible study and prayer than men do.

We are also to protect our wives emotionally as well as physically. What man would not willingly and without hesitation lay down his own life to save the lives of his wife and children? Most of us would do it instinctively, without a thought, in a moment of danger. But how about protecting them emotionally? Generally we men are created to be stronger emotionally. We don't tend to fall apart as easily or have a low point each month as many women are apt to do. God created us to see things, particularly stressful things, from a different perspective. We are to be the calming influence in the home, the shield that fends off stressful issues from our wives. But what if we are the ones causing the stress and the strain? That gives us something to think about, doesn't it!

Provider. Looking to Jesus for our example once again, we see in Ephesians 5:29 that He nourished and cherished His church and that we husbands are to regard our wives in the same way. We are to provide for their material needs, their natural needs, and their emotional needs. We are to be the bulwark they can lean on. Looking further, we see that "we are to grow up in all aspects into Him, who is the head, even Christ, from whom the whole body, being fitted and held together by that which every joint supplies, according to the proper working of each individual part" (Eph. 4:15–16 NASB). As we "grow up in all aspects into Him," we become an integral part of the supply system, and all the parts work together in harmony. This is an awesome responsibility the Father places on each of us husbands. Are we fulfilling this role He has established for us?

Presenter. Jesus desired to "present to Himself the church in all her glory, having no spot or wrinkle or any such thing; but that she should be holy and blameless" (Eph. 5:27 NASB). This scripture gives us additional insight as to how we are to regard and love our wives. Husbands are to become so Christlike that through the process and the journey of the marital union with us our wives will become spotless and "wrinkle-free." We are to create such an atmosphere in the marriage that they will be seen by the Lord as holy and blameless. This does not imply that the wife has no responsibility of her own to reach for these objectives. She surely does. The verse is only speaking of our responsibility as husbands before

the Lord. (Similarly, you might recall that the wife's instruction to be
subject to her husband only speaks of her responsibility. It speaks nothing of any authority of the husband.)

How can we mere mortals accomplish such a seemingly impossible
task? On our own, we cannot. But with the power of the risen Christ
freely flowing through our lives, our minds, and our bodies, we can make
surprising strides in that direction. This responsibility places upon us
another awesome challenge to become so "at one" with Him that we
become like Him. This means continuing our spiritual growth and maturity. Where are you today spiritually compared to where you were five
years ago? Have you made the progress you should have? Where will you
be five years from now? Determine today what your own spiritual future
will be.

Partner. In Ephesians 5 we see the repetition of the important truth
from Genesis: "a man . . . shall cleave to his wife; and the two shall
become one flesh" (v. 31 NASB). As the two of you actually become one
in flesh, in mind, in spirit, in objectives, in decisions—as you become
one in the Lord—you are truly equal partners. However, since the husband is the *head* we have the additional awesome responsibility to see
that this equal partnership becomes a reality. It is only by our leadership,
which means by our example, that this can happen. Only then will we
be fulfilled as men and our wives be fulfilled as women, for we are functioning as God intended.

It has taken many years and many mistakes, but at last Florence and I
are functioning as equal partners. We each have very definite and assigned
roles and functions. I know I am to protect her in every way I can. I know
I am to provide for her needs and desires as much as I can. I know I am
to grow up in Christ so I may provide for her a stress-free environment
where she can grow as well, holy, and blameless. I know I am to make
her feel that she is a fellow heir with me, my equal partner. And one
more thing I have learned: These are my responsibilities as her husband.
Therefore I am never to look over her shoulder and see how well she is
doing on her part! That is one responsibility God has never given me.

Is the husband the head of the wife? Scripture says yes, he is. Is the
husband the authority over the wife? Scripture never says he is. But we
do have an immense responsibility to love our wives in the same way
Christ loved the church. He loved the church so much He died for it!

Isn't it time we men wake up and retake the ground we have lost as
spiritual, emotional, and physical leaders in our families? In the following chapters specific suggestions will show you how you can become the

lawful head of your home. These are things I have done myself according to what the Scriptures have taught me, things that have made all the difference in our marriage.

14

LEARNING FROM
MY MISTAKES

On April 11, 1953, when Florence uttered those words I was waiting to hear, "I do," she made a commitment that was far deeper than she could ever imagine at that time. She thought she was signing up for a life to be lived "happily ever after." After all, she had spent hundreds of hours planning a fairy-tale wedding. Yes, my wife was indeed creative. But she had poured so much energy into creating the *wedding*, she had no time to think of the *marriage*.

When Florence said "I do" she was signing up to be first mate in the boat I was rowing. We men sit in the middle of the marriage boat and row. We have oars in both our hands, and the boat is under our control. As we leave the dock, our wife sits in the stern, gazing at us with an adoring and joyfully expectant glow, thinking she is setting out on a life-time journey of singing and strumming, laughing and loving down the beautifully forested streams of life. In the first days of this new life to-gether she may not even be aware that we didn't bring along a paddle for her to use in case we run into some rough water. We didn't *forget* to bring along that paddle for her to use. In all probability we never thought for a minute it would be needed; we never thought we would need her help. Whatever came up, we believed we could handle it.

As Florence and I look back on the years since that momentous day when we pushed off from the dock, we can see that neither of us was well prepared. There have been some years of rough waters when we could have used another paddle as a rudder or as a way to move the boat against the current when it got too strong. There have been times when our marriage needed Florence's help.

When Florence came aboard, she did so with blind and innocent trust; she didn't have a care in the world. That starry attitude lasted for perhaps forty-eight hours—until reality hit her. The wedding was over. We were now in the marriage.

I had my own case of blindness. Like most young husbands, it never occurred to me in my youthful naivete that my wife was completely entrusting her life, her future, into my hands. The decisions I would make, the courses through life that I would set, would profoundly determine whether or not she got a good deal in the choice she made when she chose me.

What an awesome burden we husbands have carried by ourselves to make our way through an often cruel and uncaring world to protect and provide for the women and children God gave us.

Our wives need us, but we need them too. Without them we are incomplete. That is God's design for the home: a husband and wife each functioning in their strengths and complementing each other in their respective weaknesses. Florence has natural abilities and gifts that I do not possess. Likewise, I am strong where she is weak. In His sovereignty God put us together to make a more perfect union.

How I regret now that I didn't invite Florence to share in the many decisions I have made in the past years of our marriage. There were many times when she was aware of and concerned about my plans or ideas. Sometimes she would tell me that she just didn't *feel* right about it. I would listen momentarily as she voiced her concerns. But when I asked her why she felt that way she usually couldn't give me a practical and rational answer. She didn't have *facts*; she only had those mysterious, intuitive feelings. And I insisted on documentation, details, and definitions.

In retrospect, it is now clear that I should have respected those feelings and heeded her advice. She was often right. But back then I hadn't learned God's principle that we should be one in mind, soul, and spirit. As the years have gone by I have become increasingly aware of the gifts, intelligence, and wisdom God has given my wife, and it has become increasingly apparent to me that I squandered many of the resources and opportunities that were available to us as a family because I didn't listen more attentively to her. Too many of the decisions, the investments of time, energy, and money, were made without consulting her. Why was I such a fool? Why didn't I see that the decisions I made alone affected her just as much as they affected me? Why did I think I had all the wisdom and all the power and didn't need her approval and agreement? How different things would have been today if I had listened, if I had known then what I know now.

This is why I share what I've learned with you, hoping you can learn from my mistakes and benefit from the insight I've gained. One of the things I always knew but never acknowledged is that my wife is bright; she has brains too! Now we discuss every significant decision together. We carefully weigh all the facets and factors, and by agreement we take no action unless we are both comfortable and content with it. We wait for the peace of Christ that gives us unanimity. Then we both accept equal responsibility for the results. Now we finally have the financial stability that eluded us when, without consulting her, I took all the actions and made all the decisions that affected our family.

I regret how long it took me to wake up, but I know I'm not the only husband who has ignored his wife's intelligence, intuition, and abilities. Many wives have told us the same kinds of problems and issues occurred in their homes. Could one of those women be *your* wife? Here's an example of a story that had a happy ending:

At a seminar a woman told us about her husband, Ben, who had his own business and who struggled to balance his time between his career and his family. He frequently talked about how, when he grew up, his dad, a pastor, "always had time for Widow Brown and her kids but never had time to watch me play baseball." But when Ben began his business he found himself wrestling with the very same priorities. It often seemed his family ranked pretty low on the list.

"I kept reminding Ben that I felt his clients were more important to him than I was. So he began scheduling time with me on his calendar, but that just made me feel like one of his clients who had an appointment. I wanted to be part of his life, not just part of his work schedule. I told him I couldn't turn our relationship on and off based on what else he had to do," she told us.

So Ben went "back to the drawing board," so to speak. He had always felt a keen awareness of God's guidance when he had business decisions to make. Now he sought God's voice on this issue, on how to make his marriage his most important priority. One day it dawned on him. He was already hearing God's voice; he just hadn't recognized it. "He realized God was trying to talk to him through me," the wife said.

"He finally made me his first priority," she said. "He began to consult me about his schedule and talk over some of the pressures he was feeling and how to balance them all out with his goals. We're partners now, even on such things as his schedule. I'm much more understanding because I know more of the details and more of the plans he has, and he is more understanding of my feelings and my abilities."

Becoming partners with your wife should be one of your goals too. We might say it should be your number-two goal after becoming a disciple, in an ever-deepening sense, of our Lord Jesus Christ. We'll talk more about this spiritual partnership in the next chapter, but here we'll focus on working together with our wives through the winds and waves, the sunshine and storms, of our years of marriage. We need their intuition, their strength, and their wisdom. The peace and happiness of our marriage largely depends on how effectively we bring them into the decision-making process. Let's look at some of the areas of our lives together where our wives' input can make a crucial difference.

Practicing Unity

The basic principle to remember in all questions about family finances, money management, or investments is *unity*. That means oneness, agreement, harmony, and a single-minded purpose. Remember the perfect harmony of the Father, the Son, and the Spirit; they are never out of perfect oneness. We can never go wrong if we first ask ourselves, "What would the Lord Jesus do? How would He handle this situation?" With this foundation in mind, let's address some of the questions about family financial issues that are frequently asked.

1. Who should pay the monthly family expenses?

The spouse who pays the bills and maintains the family checkbook should be the one who is best suited for this task, either the husband or the wife. There is no scriptural mandate as to who should be the keeper of the checkbook. It is not automatically the husband's job. Our recommendation is that it should be, first, the spouse who has the Melancholy traits, for that person will more likely see that the bills are paid on time. Second, it should be the one who enjoys math and numbers, for this person is more likely to keep the balance current and therefore not write checks for which there are no funds! Third, the keeper of the accounts should be the partner who has the time to do it or who enjoys doing it. These three criteria may all be in one and the same person!

Some couples, especially two-income families, share by prior agreement the paying of certain family obligations from their own individual incomes. For example, the husband might pay the rent or mortgage payments, the utilities, and the insurance, while the wife might pay for food, telephone, and clothing. The important thing is that the husband and wife have sat down together and planned and agreed on which expenses each one will be responsible for.

2. Should the husband and wife have separate checking accounts?

Once again, this question should be answered by agreement, not by one spouse dominating the other. If your wife feels she should have a separate account, then by all means she should have one. Many couples find they can function much more effectively with individual accounts.

Florence and I have always had separate accounts. I always make sure mine is balanced to the penny. Florence feels if she and the bank are within calling distance that's close enough! She has not balanced her checkbook in years; I have always done it for her. I try to always keep adequate funds in her account for the level of spending I know she is apt to do. She just has to let me know immediately if she has written a larger-than-usual check so we can be sure there is enough to cover it.

Our daughter Marita and her husband also have separate checking accounts. Like Florence, Marita is very Sanguine and has never been interested in trying to make all those figures agree. For the past several years she has engaged a bookkeeper to balance her account every three months. She finds it far less costly than paying the returned-check charges the bank used to deduct.

In contrast, many couples function very effectively with a single account. Checkbooks that leave a carbon copy of each check written have saved many of these couples the problems that result when one partner is forgetful about recording checks.

3. Does the husband have the right to oversee and approve his wife's spending?

If we are working under the principle laid out in Scripture, then the husband has no more right to exercise authority over his wife's spending than the wife has to exercise authority over her husband's spending. Each must have discretionary funds to spend in any way he or she chooses. The amounts of these funds should be determined beforehand by agreement and should be consistent with the couple's income and budget.

If it has been agreed that the wife is to have, for example, fifty dollars per month to spend on personal expenditures such as manicures, haircuts, luncheons with friends, or anything else she may want, then her husband has no right to second-guess how she spends that fifty dollars.

If she should choose to set aside twenty dollars each month for some special occasion, her husband should not question what she does with her little stash. She might be planning to "kidnap" him on their anniversary and take him for a weekend fling in a hotel or buy him a special surprise on his birthday! The key word here is *agree*. If you have agreed, then you both need to live up to the terms of whatever you have agreed upon.

4. What if the wife (or the husband) has compulsive spending habits and violates the agreement?

Examples of compulsive spending might be a wife who buys clothes she cannot afford in an attempt to make her feel good about herself or to try to keep up with more affluent friends. A husband might demonstrate the same unhealthy patterns by picking up the dinner check for everyone at an expensive restaurant when he could not afford to do so. His wife might wince at this act of generosity, knowing full well they will not be able to pay the charge when the credit card statement arrives. But she says nothing to avoid embarrassing her husband or incurring his wrath. The temporary solution in this case would be for the husband to acknowledge that he has a tendency to do this and turn the credit cards over to his wife until he deals with the root of this compulsive need to look good in front of his friends. The same applies to the wife with compulsive spending habits. The roots to both of these examples will usually be identified as low self-worth, a need to prove one's value. The next question to ask is where does this low self-worth come from? What are its roots? The answer will invariably come from deep feelings of rejection.

Compulsive spending is a widespread problem, and it must be dealt with quickly and honestly. The simplest way to quickly and effectively deal with it is for the non-compulsive partner, by mutual agreement, to temporarily exercise control over the family's cash and credit cards.

If compulsive spending causes problems for either of you, we strongly urge you to carefully read chapters 2, 7, and 11 in our book, *Get a Life Without the Strife*. You will quickly gain insight into the source of your feelings and learn the specific steps you can take to resolve this compulsion.

5. How do we decide about major purchases?

By now this question should be an easy one for you to answer: You do it together. Consider your need for and the worth of the prospective purchase, and evaluate your ability to pay cash for it. Most financial-management experts agree that the only things you should purchase through monthly payments are a home and a car. Be careful that even by agreement you don't allow yourselves to get caught in the trap of overbuying a home or a car to look good or to feel good.

If one of you does not feel right about the purchase or if one of you is afraid you will be unable to pay for it as planned, it is far better to postpone the purchase or kill the idea altogether than to later find yourselves in a commitment you wish you hadn't made. Maintaining the harmony of your relationship is far more important than having material possessions about which you were not in agreement. Lying awake at night because you or your wife are worried about payments is a heavy price to pay for the temporary pleasure of a new acquisition.

If you are both in agreement that the purchase is right for you and that you can afford it, follow the final and most important step: Pray, asking God to give you His peace if it is right for you to proceed. Ask Him to take away the peace from one of you if it is not His will for you. Remember God is *omniscient.* He knows you; He knows your yesterday; and He already knows your tomorrow. He knows His plans for you. He knows all! If He removes the peace from one of you, you will no longer be in agreement. "Let the peace of God *rule* in your hearts" (Col. 3:15). Without this peace you would no longer want to make the purchase, for you would be out of His will. "If you do this you will experience God's peace, which is far more wonderful than the human mind can understand" (Phil. 4:7 TLB). You have spared yourself the agony of living with the cost of a questionable decision.

6. If the husband is the sole income earner of the family shouldn't he have special rights to determine how the income will be spent or invested?

Why? Isn't the marriage a partnership? Don't the husband and wife share equally in all the assets of the marriage? Did God endow the man with any special or unique wisdom that surpasses that of his wife? Are the children of the union any more the wife's than they are the husband's? The answer to these questions must always be that the husband and wife are spiritually equal—fellow heirs of all that God bestows. As Christians we hold to the truth that "a man can receive nothing, unless it has been given him from heaven" (John 3:27 NASB). "Who regards you as superior? And what do you have that you did not receive?" (1 Cor. 4:7 NASB).

Each spouse brings his or her individual gifts to benefit the marriage. Any gifts, talents, or abilities God gives you are not for your own pleasure or blessing but for the common good of your family (see 1 Cor. 12:7 NASB). The ability to make a living, to earn an income, to receive more than you need, all these gifts were given to you that your family would receive proper provision of what is needed and then, perhaps in addition, what is desired.

There may be times when your wife will say, "I don't understand all these financial things. They're way above me. You're much better at it than I am.

I trust you to make the decisions that will be best for us as a family." In these cases a wife has given advance assent to the choices you will make. Nevertheless, you would be well advised to review with her everything you plan to do before executing the action. Not only are you keeping her informed, but you are also giving her an opportunity to ask some healthy questions and perhaps see something you may have overlooked.

Keeping your wife informed about financial matters is essential for the success of your marriage. For example, let her know what insurance coverage you have as a family, where the policies are kept, and who the agent is. Let her know what stocks or bonds the family owns, and let her see the monthly statements. If you are trading on the stock market, make sure she knows how much of the family assets you are risking. If you are successful, tell her. Ah, but how about if you make some poor choices and lose your shirt? Tell her. And in the future never risk more than the amount the two of you have agreed upon.

A word of caution and a simple test: If you have ever made an investment, loaned someone some money, or taken any other financial actions that you are afraid to tell your wife about, you have probably been outside the will of God. You have not taken advantage of the wisdom and perceptions God has given your helpmate. This is why it is so important to always discuss any major steps or decisions with your wife before acting upon them. When you act in unison, as one, you both assume equal responsibility for the success or failure or your decision.

Building Your Financial House

Jesus said, "Every one who hears these words of Mine, and does not act upon them, will be like a foolish man, who built his house upon the sand. And the rain descended, and the floods came, and the winds blew, and burst against that house; and it fell, and great was its fall" (Matt. 7:26–27 NASB). Take time now to think. How are you building your financial house? Are you building it on the sand? Will it be able to withstand the rains and the storms that will certainly come. Or are you building your house solidly on the rock of Jesus Christ? Where will you, your family, your house be ten years from now? The decisions you make today will have a profound impact on where you will be in ten years. Determine now that in the future you will always act in concert with your wife, calling upon her wisdom and the abilities God has given to her.

15

THE MARK OF A MAN

Continually restate to yourself what the purpose of your life is. The destined end of man is not happiness, nor health, but holiness. Holiness means unsullied walking with the feet, unsullied talking with the tongue, unsullied thinking with the mind—every detail of the life under the scrutiny of God.
Oswald Chambers, My Utmost for His Highest

Why are you here? What is your purpose for living? These are questions I frequently asked myself before I became a Christian in August 1966. Before then I had not a clue as to why I was on this earth. Life had not been particularly good to me; for most of my first thirty-seven years I had been plagued with doubts and discouragement even though I worked hard to overcome these barriers and become "a success." And what did I think I needed to do to become a success? Build a business, make a substantial amount of money, live in a nice house, have a loving wife and children I could be proud of, gain personal recognition, and leave this world a somewhat better place than I found it.

Look at my list again. Check the goals that apply to you and add any others that you believe indicate success.

____ Build a business.

____ Make a substantial amount of money.

____ Live in a big house.

____ Have a loving wife and children I could be proud of.

____ Gain personal recognition.

____ Leave this world a better place than I found it.

____ _____

____ _____

When I review what I once thought success meant I am struck by how materialistic and self-centered I was, with the exception of the last item on the list. And even it has self-centered overtones because I also wanted to be remembered and recognized for what I accomplished. Perhaps a statue or a publicly displayed painting would help people remember me when I was gone! I am reminded of a poem I once saw that said if you want to see how big an impact you will have on the world, stick your hand in a bucket of water then take it out. The mark that remains in the water is your mark on the world. This does tend to give one a sense of humility and finiteness! But realistically, if our purpose in life is to make our mark on the world, aren't we doomed to disappointment? After all, they toppled Lenin's statue in Red Square.

Lenin? Lenin who? How quickly they forget once we are gone.

So what *is* our purpose in this world as Christian men? Again and again Scripture gives us the clear answer:

> Let your light so shine before men, that they may see your good works, and *glorify your Father which is in heaven.* (Matt. 5:16)

> For you have been bought with a price: therefore *glorify God in your body.* (1 Cor 6:20 NASB)

> Whatever you do, *do all to the glory of God.* (1 Cor 10:31 NASB)

> With one accord you may with one voice *glorify the God and Father of our Lord Jesus Christ.* (Rom. 15:6 NASB)

Whoever speaks . . . whoever serves, let him do so as by the strength which God supplies; so that *in all things God may be glorified through Jesus Christ*. (1 Pet. 4:11 NASB)

These scriptures tell us we are put on this earth as Christian men for one thing and one thing alone: to glorify our Father in heaven. Our lives are not our own; we have been purchased with a price. Everything we do or say is to bring honor and glory to the Lord. As Oswald Chambers so eloquently wrote, "The purpose for which [we are] created is that [we] may be God's servant, one in whom God is glorified."[1] He also wrote, "There is only one relationship that matters, and that is your personal relationship to a personal Redeemer and Lord. Let everything else go, but maintain that at all costs, and God will fulfill His purpose through your life."[2]

The Relationship That Matters Most

To help you evaluate how well you are letting everything else go so you can concentrate on the "one relationship that matters," write the number that best describes your response now, *today*, to each verse in the following evaluation.

> 0 = Rarely
> 1 = Sometimes
> 2 = Often
> 3 = Most of the time

Don't be afraid to write a three if your answer really is "most of the time." But also be honest enough to give yourself a zero if you rarely do as this verse directs you. No one is going to check up on you. Your answers are for you alone to help you assess your current spiritual commitment.

_____ 1. "Seek ye first the kingdom of God, and His righteousness." (Matt. 6:33)

_____ 2. "Do not lay up for yourselves treasures upon earth . . . . But lay up for yourselves treasures in heaven." (Matt. 6:19–20 NASB)

_____ 3. Devote yourselves to prayer, keeping *alert* in it with an attitude of thanksgiving. (Col. 4:2 NASB)

_____ 4. Accept one another [including your wife], just as Christ also accepted [you] to the glory of God. (Rom. 15:7 NASB)

_____ 5. Be kind to one another, tender-hearted, forgiving each other, just as God in Christ also has forgiven you. (Eph. 4:32 NASB)

_____ 6. Husbands, love your wives, just as Christ also loved the church and gave Himself up for her. (Eph. 5:25 NASB)

_____ 7. Do nothing from selfishness but . . . regard [your wife] as more important than [yourself]. (Phil. 2:3 NASB)

_____ 8. Rejoice always; pray without ceasing; in _everything_ give thanks. (1 Thess. 5:16–18 NASB)

_____ 9. Whatever is true, whatever is honorable, whatever is right, whatever is pure, whatever is lovely, . . . _let your mind dwell_ on these things. (Phil. 4:8 NASB)

_____ 10. Discipline yourself for the _purpose of godliness_; for bodily discipline is only of little profit, but godliness is profitable for all things, . . . for the present life and also for the life to come. (1 Tim. 4:7–8 NASB)

_____ 11. Let no unwholesome word proceed from your mouth, but only such . . . that it may give grace [a favor] to those who hear. (Eph. 4:29 NASB)

_____ 12. Lay aside every encumbrance, and the sin which so easily entangles us, and . . . run with endurance the race that is set before us, fixing our eyes on Jesus. (Heb. 12:1–2 NASB)

Now add up all your responses and enter your total score: _____

The maximum score on your spiritual evaluation is thirty-six. How did you rate yourself? If you were a little too hard on yourself go back and recheck your answers. On the other hand, if you gave yourself a higher score than you know you deserve go back and correct that as well. Be honest with yourself. The objective is to help you see how deeply you are committed to becoming like Him and how effectively you are working to have that "mind in you, which was also in Christ Jesus" (Phil. 2:5).

That should be our goal, our purpose in life. As we become more and more like Him, we take into ourselves more and more of His nature and characteristics. Our friends begin to see the difference. Our family members start to feel more relaxed and comfortable around us. They begin to see a new kind of husband and father, one whose life radiates the love of the Lord Jesus.

Did you end up with a total score below twenty? A score in this range indicates that living for the Lord and making Him preeminent in your life is probably not your highest priority right now. Other things are capturing your time and attention. They may all be "good" things. They may not be bad or evil. But they may not be the "best" things you could be focusing on. You now have the opportunity to decide what will be the centerpiece, the focus, of your life in the future. Where will you be spiritually a year from today? Write down your answer in the space below.

I determine today that a year from now I will _____

_____

_____.

If your total score falls between twenty-one and thirty, you are clearly making a conscientious effort to become the man that God intends you to be. You can see for yourself where your lower scores were and gain insight into the areas where you need to apply some extra attention and effort.

Scores between thirty-one and thirty-six don't mean you're almost perfect. So don't pat yourself on the back just yet! Let the Lord Jesus tell you when He is well pleased with you. But scores in this range do help you see that you are moving in the direction He desires for you.

"The abiding characteristic of a spiritual man is . . . the one concentrated *passion* of the life is *Jesus Christ*," wrote Oswald Chambers. "Never allow anything to deflect you from insight into Jesus Christ. It is the test of whether you are spiritual or not. To be unspiritual means that other things have a growing fascination for you."[3]

How to Become More Spiritual

As Christians we understand that we are to make the Lord the first priority in our lives. But the question is always how do we actually do that? How do we find time for Him in the day? You may be saying what I said a few years ago: "My day is already so full, I don't even have time for myself."

Sometimes it's not easy to change old habits, even when we know how important it is to make the change. But there is one certainty, no matter how busy our days are, no matter how pressured we already feel our lives are: We must make time for the Lord. We must make Him the first priority in every day of our lives.

There are at least three constants in our lives. One is aging and eventually death. Another is change, or uncertainty. The third is time: We all have the same twenty-four hours in every day and, to varying degrees, the discretion to determine how we use that amount of time.

If we are to be the spiritual leaders of our homes, if we are to fulfill our God-ordained function of responsibility as Scripture directs us, we must make a commitment. We must find a minimum of thirty minutes a day when we can be alone with God. Our goal should be an hour, but we can start with a more modest objective. Look over your daily schedule. When can you set aside at least thirty minutes to spend with Him? It might mean getting up a half-hour earlier or setting aside part of your lunch hour. It might mean missing your favorite television program or getting ready for bed a half-hour earlier and then retreating to the quiet spot you have set aside for your daily communion.

There are two essential elements of the Christian's daily life. Both are equally important, but tragically most men omit them completely from their daily lives. These two essentials are Bible study and prayer.

Bible Study

How much time have you actually spent in Bible study, not in church or in a group but in *personal* Bible study, in the past seven days? Count up the actual number of minutes or hours you have spent in undistracted prayer with your Father in heaven during these same seven days. The minutes or hours you come up with will probably closely correlate to your score on the spiritual assessment. Why do we men so often allow our wives to surpass us in Bible study, in seminars, in personal growth—and then expect them to recognize and accept us as their spiritual "head"?

I would like you to know that I, too, struggled for many years with these same conflicts. Bible study was never really a problem for me. I enjoyed studying, learning, and growing in my knowledge of God's Word. The problem was finding the time to do it. Too frequently the pressures of my daily schedule, the "tyranny of the urgent," would crowd out my best intentions; weeks, maybe months, would go by before I realized I had been skipping my daily Bible study.

Prayer

While Bible study is something I've always enjoyed, the other daily essential, prayer, was a different matter for me. It never seemed to come easily, perhaps because no one ever taught me how to pray. Too often when I would sit at my desk to pray my mind would begin wandering. Other times I would start to pray and then just doze off. I tried praying in a corner. I tried praying on my knees. I tried praying standing up. I tried praying in the car while driving to work. Nothing seemed to work. Because prayer seemed to be so unmeaningful, I pretty much stopped praying except at appointed times.

Until about six years ago I could count up on one hand the number of meaningful times of prayer I had experienced in my whole Christian life! All that has changed, and now I often speak on prayer, sharing what I've learned. I begin by asking, "How many of you, like me, have struggled with prayer? Do you find that your mind wanders or you doze off, and then because prayer seems not to be meaningful to you, you find yourself not praying very much?" No longer am I stunned at the number of hands raised in response to my questions—usually a full 80 percent of the audience! So I know this is a common problem. It is particularly a problem for people who have suffered childhood victimization. Among those of us who have been violated it is almost universal!

Six years ago all I needed was one hand to count the times when prayer had stirred my heart. But today? There have been too many times to count! Sometimes it is daily, one wonderful day after another. I admit that some days my prayer time doesn't seem to be as dynamic as on other days. But that isn't the issue, for I am still maintaining my daily prayer contact with my Father in heaven. I look forward each day to the time we spend together. Bible study is still rewarding and insightful; now prayer is too. What has made the difference? It's a practice I began six years ago.

16

THE LIFE-CHANGING
POWER OF PRAYER

The effectual fervent prayer of a righteous man availeth much.

James 5:16

In the last chapter I shared with you how Bible study and prayer have helped me become more spiritual, more attuned to God's will for my life. And I promised to share with you how my prayers had evolved from being aimless mutterings marred by endless distractions, drowsiness, and lack of focus to becoming life-changing times of close, one-on-one communion with God. At first glance, what I'm about to tell you may seem incredibly simple. But I assure you, if you do what I suggest consistently, with your heart and mind open to God's presence, it can change your life.

Six years ago I began, at the Lord's direction, to write down my daily prayers. I've done it almost every day since then. I simply write a letter to my Father in heaven, sometimes addressing Him as "Dear Lord Jesus," other times as "Dear Heavenly Father." There are times when I don't address Him at all; I just start writing to Him. The words and the form are not important. What is important is that I come into His presence to talk to Him, praise Him, worship Him, confess to Him, ask of Him, and to intercede before Him for someone else. Over the last six years I have spent an average of thirty to forty minutes in communion with Him each day. There have been many times when we have spent well over an hour together.

Until March 1993 I used a standard-size 8 1/2" x 11" spiral notebook. (Later I'll tell you what I use now.) Writing on both sides of the page, two hundreds pages or more per notebook, I have filled thirteen notebooks. I call them my "prayer closet." I always have my current notebook with me, and wherever I am, whenever the time presents itself, I sequester myself away and spend personal, private time with the Lord.

The Blessings of Daily Written Prayer

Writing your prayers does many things for you. In my life, the most obvious thing it has done is bring me the healing power of the Lord. All the old issues I struggled with for so many years have been cleansed away. Today when I speak on how prayer can change your life, there are always people who come up to me later and tell me the phenomenal changes that have occurred in their lives, too, as they have written their prayers.

Writing your prayers is also an important discipline; by dating your prayers you can see very quickly if you have missed any days. Second, it helps you focus your mind on the Lord and prevents your thoughts from wandering. Writing also helps keep you alert, in accordance with Colossians 4:2: "Devote yourselves to prayer, keeping alert in it with an attitude of thanksgiving" (NASB).

It also helps protect you from the flaming missiles of the evil one, who is very happy when Christians are not praying. Inevitably he tries to attack us as we endeavor to submit ourselves to the Lord and draw closer to Him.

Most amazingly, as I write my prayers, I have learned to hear God's still, small voice. When I do I write down exactly, word for word, what He has said to me!

This describes only a fraction of the many blessings I have been given by coming to my heavenly Father in daily written prayer. If you are interested in further understanding of written prayer I suggest you read my book *The Promise of Healing*.[1] The final section is devoted to various practical aspects of making written prayer, or prayer journaling as it is also called, a rewarding part of your daily journey with the Lord.

Perhaps the most significant benefit of daily written prayer is a totally changed life! For verification that it has changed my life, you could ask my wife. She lives with me. She sees that the suppressed anger that once raged within me is gone. She no longer sees a critical spirit in me. Now she not only enjoys being with me, she misses me deeply on those few occasions when we're apart. Jesus said, "I have come to heal the brokenhearted, to set the captive free" (paraphrase of Luke 4:18). He has done that for me through written prayer simply because I was obedient to His offer to "Come unto me, all ye that labour and are heavy laden, and I will give you rest" (Matt. 11:28). God also kept the promise made in Isaiah 26:3: "Thou wilt keep him in perfect peace, whose mind is stayed on thee." Writing my prayers enables me to keep my mind focused, or "stayed on" Him.

I will never forget an experience that happened just a few years ago when I started to write my prayers early one morning. I had begun my prayers with an inspiring time of Bible study. Then I started to write. I wrote and wrote, covering about four and a half pages. I didn't have any particular issues that morning to discuss with my Father; I was just enjoying our fellowship. When I finished after an hour and twenty minutes of writing I felt uplifted, encouraged, and filled with His Spirit. Then I decided to read over again, for a second blessing, the prayers I had just written. How long do you think it took me to read what I had just spent well over an hour writing? Just about four minutes!

Then I heard a voice speaking to me. It sounded so clear in my mind I will never forget the exact words I heard: "You're wasting your time writing your prayers. Think of how many more people you could pray for if you prayed orally." It sounded logical and seemed valid, but immediately I heard another voice, a different one say, "No, I want you to continue writing your prayers, for all the time you are writing your mind is stayed on Me!" There was no question whose voices I heard. The second was clearly the Lord, countermanding the voice of satan. He was trying to separate me from what the Lord was using to bring me closer to Him. I don't know about you, but as for me and my house, we will serve the Lord! I will not listen to the evil one.

I have continued to write my prayers almost daily since that time. I say *almost* for there have been days when I've missed this communion. I have learned how important it is, however, to *not miss* because if I miss but one day, it seems quite easy to miss another. And if I happen to miss two, well missing just one more will be OK, won't it? No, it won't! That's just what satan is watching for. He wants me to miss; then he knows I may become vulnerable so his fiery darts are more apt to sneak through my spiritual armor.

Maintaining Daily Discipline

I have developed a little system that helps me maintain the daily discipline of writing my prayers. It may also help you maintain good habits and can be used just as effectively to help you break bad ones. Each day in a small pocket diary I write down the number of how many days in a row I have spent time with the Lord in written prayer. There have been days when I wasn't able to get to my prayer time until late at night because of the complexity of our schedule that day. Now I will not allow myself to get in bed until I have had at least some time with the Lord. I'll admit I'm apt to be sleepy, and my prayer time may be a little shorter than usual or less intense than I would like, but I still take a moment to bring my spirit into communion with God. It's not that God needs to hear from me. It's that I need that time with Him, and I can't afford to miss even one day. Tomorrow might be just as hectic, and then I would have missed two! As I see that little number growing each day on my weekly diary, I don't want to have to go back to zero and start all over. It really works to give me that edge that I need in self-discipline. And the results speak for themselves!

In March of 1993 I succumbed to the temptation of buying a lap-top computer. Even though I was basically "computer illiterate" I began learning how to write my daily prayers on my computer. I'm still not a typist, but I'm getting there; gradually, I'm picking up my writing speed. Now instead of getting cramps in my arms I sometimes get them in my shoulders! Writing my prayers on my lap-top computer has proved to be just as effective as handwriting, but it gives me many additional technical advantages. It has now become my new prayer closet where I pray to my Father who hears me in secret and rewards me openly (see Matt. 6:6).

We are all well aware that there are many scriptures that command us to pray. We know that prayer is for our benefit, not God's. The Lord doesn't need to hear our prayers, but He likes to hear from us. He wants to hear from us. Jesus, Himself, in His earthly ministry, frequently slipped away to a private place to pray to His Father. In the garden at Gethsemane on the night before His crucifixion, Jesus went a little way away from Peter, James, and John and said to them, "Remain here and keep watch with Me." When He returned about an hour later, what were they doing? They were sleeping! He was about to give His life for them, and they couldn't even stay awake to stand watch while He prayed! His words to them are still important for us to understand today: "So, *you men could not keep watch with Me for one hour?*" Is Jesus saying something to you at this very moment about keeping watch with Him for just one hour? Perhaps just one hour a day? His very next words to these three disciples are equally significant for us, His disciples today. "Keep watching and praying, that you may not enter into temptation; the spirit is willing, but the flesh is weak" (see Matt. 26:36–42, Mark 14:32–38, and Luke 22:40 NASB).

How profound His words are for us today. Indeed, our spirit is willing, but there is so much temptation around us. It is so easy to stumble—not only to stumble into sin but far more frequently to stumble out of our daily prayer fellowship with Him. Make no mistake, satan lurks about like a roaring lion, seeking whom he may devour (see 1 Pet. 5:8). It is a foolish general who does not keep his or her perimeters well armed and guarded. It is a foolish Christian who does not keep his or her spiritual defenses on full-time alert, as well, always vigilant, ever ready to discern the infiltrations of the enemy. Those flaming missiles will come as surely as the darkness descends at the end of each day.

Staying consistently close to the source of our spiritual power enables us to know exactly where our shield of faith is so we can reach for it in time to protect ourselves and our family from the enemy's attacks! Our Father expects us to be the *protectors* of our families, protecting them physically and emotionally, and certainly as spiritual leaders we are to protect them spiritually. To do this we need to know the strength of our spiritual power, and we need to know how to exercise it.

Exercising Our Spiritual Power

Most of us have little to no idea of the powerful resources available to us as Christians to stand against the wicked and evil forces of darkness. That they exist is not in question, for Scripture specifically tells us "we wrestle not against flesh and blood, but against *principalities*, against *powers*, against the *rulers* of the darkness of this world, against spiritual wickedness in high places" (Eph. 6:12).

That we will have the victory over these evil powers is abundantly clear, for we are told to resist the devil and he *will* flee from us (see James 4:7). He has no choice; he must flee. He must obey when we exercise the power the Lord Jesus gave to everyone who has volunteered to serve in His army.

That we already have the needed weapons to resist him is also abundantly clear. "The weapons of our warfare are not of the flesh, . . . but [are] divinely powerful for the destruction of fortresses" (2 Cor. 10:5). Note the masculine fortitude of the words in this verse: *weapons . . . warfare . . . powerful . . . fortresses.* It is not by our manly physical strength, for how can we strike out at something we cannot see? "Not by might, nor by power, but by my spirit, saith the LORD" (Zech. 4:6). It is real men, Christian men, holy men, men who are leaders in fact not only in title, men who will go forward without hesitation—these are the men who are needed to protect their families, to stand up against the wiles and forces of the enemy.

A battle is raging. It is an unseen spiritual battle that must be waged continuously on all fronts. But it is a battle in which we are *always assured of victory!*

This is such a crucial point I'd like you to be able to see it directly in Scripture. Take a moment, now, and get your Bible. We'll look together at something many Christians have never noticed. I know your tendency is to stay where you are and just read over this material, thinking you'll look up the Bible references later. But please do it *now*.

Turn to Luke 9:1 and read about the special empowerment the Lord gave His disciples. What were "the power and authority" He gave them? At this point they seem to be apostolic gifts given uniquely to the Twelve.

Now look at Luke 10:1. How many did He appoint? (Note that some original manuscripts indicate seventy, and some say seventy-two. I happen to believe the correct figure is seventy-two; I'll explain why in a moment. It's quite fascinating.) Next look at verse 17. What does it say? What were the seventy-two exclaiming when they returned?

"Lord, even the demons are subject to us in Your name."(NASB)

We have clearly seen that the Lord gave the very same power to the seventy-two as He gave to the Twelve! The key to this whole passage appears in verses 19 and 20. To whom did He give this power? And what was the specific power He gave them?

"Behold, I have given you [power and] authority[2] to tread upon serpents[3] and scorpions,[4] and over all the power of the enemy, and nothing shall injure you . . . The spirits are subject to you." (NASB)

We might slightly modify this passage this way to more clearly understand the symbolic metaphors and the amazing empowerment He has given to us: "Pay careful attention! I have given you My power and authority over satan and his demons and over all the power of the enemy. There is nothing they can do to you, for even the spirits are subject to you in My name."

So let me ask again, who is He giving this power to? Realize that these seventy-two are unnamed. Therefore, this is no longer an apostolic gift.

Now it gets even more interesting. In Luke 9:1 the gift was given to the Twelve; in Luke 10:1 it is given to an additional nonspecified seventy-two. Now how many have received the gift? The first twelve plus seventy-two more equals eighty-four. Think back to your high school math. What are the two lowest common denominators that when multiplied together will equal eighty-four?

The answers are seven and twelve. Seven times twelve equals eighty-four. As you are no doubt aware, numbers are very significant in the Scriptures. Seven is described as God's number of completion, fullness, and abundance, and twelve as God's number of divine administration. Eighty-four then may be considered to represent the *fullness of God's divine administration.* This is the evidence for my belief that the number mentioned in Luke 10:1 is seventy-two.

Why is this so important to you and me? Very simply because it shows that this awesome empowerment was not given just to the apostles, not just to these nonspecified seventy-two, but to *all* who belong to the Lord Jesus Christ, who are a part of His divine administration. He has already given to you and to me all the power and authority we need over satan! Once we hold this knowledge firmly secure it remains only for us to exercise this God-given power.

And we exercise it exactly as Jesus did. For a review of some of the key passages describing how Jesus demonstrated this power against satan and demons, study these verses:

Matthew 4:10, 8:32, 9:33, and 17:18
Mark 1:25
Luke 4:36, 41
See also Acts 8:7 and 16:18

We speak out with authority, the authority He has already given us. The next time you sense something is amiss in your home, in your heart, or with your family, particularly in emotional issues for this is where satan loves to attack us, stop and simply pray the following prayer, or something similar. The exact words are not important. What is important is that, as the head of your household, you exercise the spiritual power that has been given to you and that you exercise it in the name of the Lord Jesus Christ. In Him you have all power over satan! By yourself, you have NONE. Say the prayer out loud; don't read it silently. Satan probably cannot read your mind, but he definitely can hear your voice!

> *Satan, in the name of the Lord Jesus Christ, I take authority over you. I rebuke you. I bind you.*
> *I command you to leave this place.*
> *I command you to leave me.*
> *You are not permitted to interfere in my life.*
> *Satan, in the name and through the blood of the Lord Jesus Christ, I tell you and all your evil spirits to be gone!*
> *Be gone from here!*

If you have never prayed like this before, you will be thrilled and astounded at the peace and freedom that comes over you. When you finish, it would be appropriate to thank the One who gave you this power:

> *Lord Jesus, I thank You for the power You have given to me over satan.*
> *I thank You that he must obey me.*
> *I thank You for the freedom You have given me.*
> *Now, dear Lord, I ask You to fill me with Your Holy Spirit and give me Your perfect peace.*
> *Lord Jesus, I thank You, I praise You, and I worship You. Amen.*

Keep a copy of these suggested prayers in a handy place. When you have the opportunity to use the prayer to rebuke satan (and there will be plenty of these times), don't hesitate to do so. You will be amazed at how quickly this aggressive enemy will flee when you invoke the name of the Lord Jesus Christ.

Prayer is powerful. In so many ways, it can change your life. It can also change the lives of those you love.

The Amazing Power of Intercessory Prayer

Trish, a friend of ours, wrote to us, saying, "There is nothing more powerful, more influential, more effective than taking our loved ones to the almighty God through intercessory prayer." You'll see why she's such a believer when you read her story:

> After twelve-step programs, "tough love," and residential teatment programs failed to help my daughter break her devastating, three-year addiction to crystal methamphetamine the courts ordered her to be under house arrest in my home. It seemed the court had given me one last chance to save this child I loved so much, and after enduring what had seemed like three years of hell on earth, I had no one else but God to turn to for help. I put my trust in Him to bring Jana back from the brink.
>
> I prayed frequently during Jana's time of confinement with us, and during one of those prayers the Lord very clearly spoke to my heart, telling me Jana was using drugs to medicate the pain of her past. He told me Jana needed *unconditional* love,

something I was only able to give when I started seeing her through His eyes. Then God reminded me it wasn't enough to tell Jana I loved her; I had to *show* her. I was to model Christ to her. But I realized the only way I could take on His characteristics was by being close to Him and spending time with Him in prayer and in reading His Word.

So I started reading my one-year Bible; it's the *New International Version*. I had been a Christian all my life, but I had never read the Bible cover-to-cover. I started receiving help and guidance right away. Early in my Scripture reading I was reminded (in Exodus 6:7), "You will know that I am the LORD your God." Then Matthew 18:35 told me not to be judgmental and to forgive Jana on a daily basis.

In February I read Exodus 14:14: "The LORD will fight for you; you need only to be still," and Psalm 27:14 told me, "Wait for the LORD; be strong and take heart." I began to realize this was not a physical battle, but a battle against "principalities, against powers, against the rulers of the darkness of this world, against spiritual wickedness in high places" (Eph. 6:12 KJV).

Mark 1:35 told me Jesus got up early in the morning and went to a solitary place to pray. Modeling His ways, I did the same, often praying Psalm 51 specifically for Jana: "Have mercy on my daughter, O God . . . Wash away all her iniquity and cleanse her from her sin. For You know her transgressions, and her sin is always before her." This was the psalm God had given me for Jana several years earlier. So it was a special joy as I continued through the one-year Bible and came to Psalm 51 on Jana's birthday! I was astonished and in awe of our Lord. I showed the psalm to Jana, and I reminded her I would *never stop praying for her.*

In March I read Proverbs 10:3 "The LORD . . . thwarts the craving of the wicked," and I prayed, "Lord, thwart Jana's cravings for drugs." Then I came to the passage in Mark 7:25–30 that describes the mother who asked Jesus to drive the demon out of her daughter. I got down on my knees and begged Jesus to drive the demon out of Jana. I pleaded her case before God Almighty, and I knew beyond a shadow of a doubt that Jesus would free my daughter.

By that time, the court had released Jana from house arrest and once again she left our home. I was devastated to learn within a few weeks that she was using illicit drugs again. One afternoon I stood in my kitchen, my heart heavy with despair, and cried out, "Lord, save her!" In the quietness of my soul He responded, "Trish, wait upon Me. I shall renew your strength; you will soar on wings like eagles. You shall run and not grow weary. You will walk and not be faint" (see Isa. 40:31). I remembered that eagles do not fly on their own; the wind picks them up. All they have to do is stretch out their wings and the wind does the rest!

Even though the circumstances looked like a defeat, I continued to pray scripture after scripture on Jana's behalf. I took on the "full armor of God" (Eph. 6:11). I vowed to fight this battle by praying God's Word and thus wielding the sword of the Spirit.

Everywhere I went I carried with me a little book of the Scriptures compiled by Lee Roberts, *Praying God's Will for My Daughter*. This was such an easy but powerful way to pray!

My heart broke as Jana kept running from God, but He reminded me to *never give up!* I read Proverbs 13:4: "The sluggard craves and gets nothing, but the desires of the diligent are fully satisfied." Heeding this advice, I remained diligent in my prayers, and soon they were answered.

In April my daughter called me and said she had been clean for two weeks. An old boyfriend who had moved to another city had come to visit her and, seeing that she was using drugs again, had insisted that she leave her deadly environment. He took her home with him to stay at his parents' house. Jana told me something important had happened to her there. She had prayed to God and asked Him what He needed to do in her so she could do His will. And then, she said, "I got this weird feeling and started shaking all over. Then I vomited as I have never done before; it was awful. It came from deep, deep inside me. I could hardly breathe. And then it was gone. Mom, I vomited up the demon inside me. Suddenly I knew the demon was gone! I felt free! I felt an overwhelming presence of the Lord, and I felt His peace. My friend felt it too!"

Listening to Jana, I suddenly remembered Jesus' words in Luke 18:27: "What is impossible with men is possible with God."

That was nearly a year ago. My daughter has been drug-free since then; the craving for drugs is gone. People ask me, "What will you do if she goes back to her old lifestyle?" All I know for sure is that I will never stop praying Scripture for her and trusting God to help her grow in His image. He has shown me His almighty hand and His glory. Nothing will take that away!"

Are You Ready to Change Your Life?

Your life *can* change. It can become the satisfying, spiritually abundant life God planned for you. But *you* have to make the changes happen—not in others, but in yourself. *You* have to take the initiative, find the time, and do the work. And you can only succeed with God's help.

In this book, I've honestly shared the problems I've endured (and caused!), and I've described the cleansing restoration I've received with God's powerful help. I've shown you how I'm working to grow into being the spiritual, emotional, and physical leader of my family that Scripture mandates. Now that I've been cleansed of that old, emotional baggage I used to drag around, I'm living a life full of joy and marked by love. I feel I've been freed to share, with the woman God created to be my helpmate, a renewed life that's packed down and running over with rich meaning, spiritual fulfillment, and God-inspired love.

Are you ready for this kind of life? Begin with prayer. Write it down. Pour it out. Thank God for your life, your family, the opportunities you've been given. Thank Him for this second chance to make things right. Ask Him to help you see yourself, to examine your life, then confess those things that must be forgiven. Next, open your heart to God's cleansing and healing, and open your mind and your ears to those around you, those closest to you. Really listen! Find out where you need to make changes in your life. Then ask God to help you make them. If you ask Him, He will help you. It may not be easy, but the results will be worth whatever it takes. And if you've read this far, you've surely overcome the first and probably the biggest obstacle.

You've told yourself, "Wake up!"

APPENDIX A

PERSONALITY PROFILE TEST

Directions: In *each* of the following rows of *four words across* place an X in front of the <u>one</u> word that most often applies to you. Continue through all forty lines. Be sure each numbered line is marked. If you are not sure which word most applies, ask a spouse or a friend, or think of what your answer would have been *when you were a child*. These forms and charts were included in *Get a Life Without the Strife* (Thomas Nelson, 1993). Some forms, where noted, were originally published elsewhere.

Strengths

1. ___ Adventurous	___ Adaptable	___ Animated	___ Analytical
2. ___ Persistent	___ Playful	___ Persuasive	___ Peaceful
3. ___ Submissive	___ Self-sacrificing	___ Sociable	___ Strong-willed
4. ___ Considerate	___ Controlled	___ Competitive	___ Convincing
5. ___ Refreshing	___ Respectful	___ Reserved	___ Resourceful
6. ___ Satisfied	___ Sensitive	___ Self-reliant	___ Spirited
7. ___ Planner	___ Patient	___ Positive	___ Promoter
8. ___ Sure	___ Spontaneous	___ Scheduled	___ Shy
9. ___ Orderly	___ Obliging	___ Outspoken	___ Optimistic
10. ___ Friendly	___ Faithful	___ Funny	___ Forceful
11. ___ Daring	___ Delightful	___ Diplomatic	___ Detailed
12. ___ Cheerful	___ Consistent	___ Cultured	___ Confident
13. ___ Idealistic	___ Independent	___ Inoffensive	___ Inspiring
14. ___ Demonstrative	___ Decisive	___ Dry humor	___ Deep
15. ___ Mediator	___ Musical	___ Mover	___ Mixes easily
16. ___ Thoughtful	___ Tenacious	___ Talker	___ Tolerant
17. ___ Listener	___ Loyal	___ Leader	___ Lively
18. ___ Contented	___ Chief	___ Chartmaker	___ Cute
19. ___ Perfectionist	___ Pleasant	___ Productive	___ Popular
20. ___ Bouncy	___ Bold	___ Behaved	___ Balanced

Weaknesses

21.	___ Blank	___ Bashful	___ Brassy	___ Bossy
22.	___ Undisciplined	___ Unsympathetic	___ Unenthusiastic	___ Unforgiving
23.	___ Reticent	___ Resentful	___ Resistant	___ Repetitious
24.	___ Fussy	___ Fearful	___ Forgetful	___ Frank
25.	___ Impatient	___ Insecure	___ Indecisive	___ Interrupts
26.	___ Unpopular	___ Uninvolved	___ Unpredictable	___ Unaffectionate
27.	___ Headstrong	___ Haphazard	___ Hard-to-please	___ Hesitant
28.	___ Plain	___ Pessimistic	___ Proud	___ Permissive
29.	___ Angers easily	___ Aimless	___ Argumentative	___ Alienated
30.	___ Naive	___ Negative attitude	___ Nervy	___ Nonchalant
31.	___ Worrier	___ Withdrawn	___ Workaholic	___ Wants credit
32.	___ Too sensitive	___ Tactless	___ Timid	___ Talkative
33.	___ Doubtful	___ Disorganized	___ Domineering	___ Depressed
34.	___ Inconsistent	___ Introvert	___ Intolerant	___ Indifferent
35.	___ Messy	___ Moody	___ Mumbles	___ Manipulative
36.	___ Slow	___ Stubborn	___ Show-off	___ Skeptical
37.	___ Loner	___ Lord over others	___ Lazy	___ Loud
38.	___ Sluggish	___ Suspicious	___ Short-tempered	___ Scatterbrained
39.	___ Revengeful	___ Restless	___ Reluctant	___ Rash
40.	___ Compromising	___ Critical	___ Crafty	___ Changeable

Now transfer all your Xs to the corresponding words on the Personality Profile Scoring Form, giving one point for each X; then add up your totals.

Personality Scoring Form

Place an X beside the corresponding words you marked on the Personality Profile Test. Then, giving one point for each X, add up your totals.

Strengths

	Popular Sanguine	Powerful Choleric	Perfect Melancholy	Peaceful Phlegmatic
1.	___ Animated	___ Adventurous	___ Analytical	___ Adaptable
2.	___ Playful	___ Persuasive	___ Persistent	___ Peaceful
3.	___ Sociable	___ Strong-willed	___ Self-sacrificing	___ Submissive
4.	___ Convincing	___ Competitive	___ Considerate	___ Controlled
5.	___ Refreshing	___ Resourceful	___ Respectful	___ Reserved
6.	___ Spirited	___ Self-reliant	___ Sensitive	___ Satisfied
7.	___ Promoter	___ Positive	___ Planner	___ Patient
8.	___ Spontaneous	___ Sure	___ Scheduled	___ Shy
9.	___ Optimistic	___ Outspoken	___ Orderly	___ Obliging
10.	___ Funny	___ Forceful	___ Faithful	___ Friendly
11.	___ Delightful	___ Daring	___ Detailed	___ Diplomatic
12.	___ Cheerful	___ Confident	___ Cultured	___ Consistent
13.	___ Inspiring	___ Independent	___ Idealistic	___ Inoffensive
14.	___ Demonstrative	___ Decisive	___ Deep	___ Dry humor
15.	___ Mixes easily	___ Mover	___ Musical	___ Mediator
16.	___ Talker	___ Tenacious	___ Thoughtful	___ Tolerant
17.	___ Lively	___ Leader	___ Loyal	___ Listener
18.	___ Cute	___ Chief	___ Chartmaker	___ Contented
19.	___ Popular	___ Productive	___ Perfectionist	___ Pleasant
20.	___ Bouncy	___ Bold	___ Behaved	___ Balanced

Subtotals

___   ___   ___   ___

Weaknesses

21. ___ Brassy	___ Bossy	___ Bashful	___ Blank
22. ___ Undisciplined	___ Unsympathetic	___ Unforgiving	___ Unenthusiastic
23. ___ Repetitious	___ Resistant	___ Resentful	___ Reticent
24. ___ Forgetful	___ Frank	___ Fussy	___ Fearful
25. ___ Interrupts	___ Impatient	___ Insecure	___ Indecisive
26. ___ Unpredictable	___ Unaffectionate	___ Unpopular	___ Uninvolved
27. ___ Haphazard	___ Headstrong	___ Hard-to-please	___ Hesitant
28. ___ Permissive	___ Proud	___ Pessimistic	___ Plain
29. ___ Angers easily	___ Argumentative	___ Alienated	___ Aimless
30. ___ Naive	___ Nervy	___ Negative attitude	___ Nonchalant
31. ___ Wants credit	___ Workaholic	___ Withdrawn	___ Worrier
32. ___ Talkative	___ Tactless	___ Too sensitive	___ Timid
33. ___ Disorganized	___ Domineering	___ Depressed	___ Doubtful
34. ___ Inconsistent	___ Intolerant	___ Introvert	___ Indifferent
35. ___ Messy	___ Manipulative	___ Moody	___ Mumbles
36. ___ Show-off	___ Stubborn	___ Skeptical	___ Slow
37. ___ Loud	___ Lord over others	___ Loner	___ Lazy
38. ___ Scatterbrained	___ Short-tempered	___ Suspicious	___ Sluggish
39. ___ Restless	___ Rash	___ Revengeful	___ Reluctant
40. ___ Changeable	___ Crafty	___ Critical	___ Compromising

___   ___   ___   ___

(Column Subtotals)

___   ___   ___   ___

Grand totals

The following table shows how the typical strengths and weaknesses of the personality types are revealed emotionally, with friends, and at work.

Table 1
Comparison of Strengths and Weaknesses by Personality Type

STRENGTHS

	Popular Sanguine	Powerful Choleric	Perfect Melancholy	Peaceful Phlegmatic
E M O T I O N S	Appealing personality Talkative, storyteller Life of the party Good sense of humor Memory for color Physically holds on to listener Emotional and demonstrative Enthusiastic and expressive Cheerful and bubbling over Curious Good on stage Wide-eyed and innocent Lives in the present Changeable disposition Sincere at heart Always a child	Born leader Dynamic and active Compulsive need for change Must correct wrongs Strong-willed and decisive Unemotional Not easily discouraged Independent and self-sufficient Exudes confidence Can run anything	Deep and thoughtful Analytical Serious and purposeful Genius prone Talented and creative Artistic or musical Philosophical and poetic Appreciative of beauty Sensitive to others Self-sacrificing Conscientious Idealistic	Low-key personality Easygoing and relaxed Calm, cool, and collected Patient, well-balanced Consistent life Quiet, but witty Sympathetic and kind Keeps emotions hidden Happily reconciled to life All-purpose person
W O R K	Volunteers for jobs Thinks up new activities Looks great on the surface Creative and colorful Has energy and enthusiasm Starts in a flash way Inspires others to join Charms others to work	Goal-oriented Sees the whole picture Organizes well Seeks practical solutions Moves quickly to action Delegates work Insists on production Makes the goal Stimulates activity Thrives on opposition	Schedule-oriented Perfectionist, high standards Detail-conscious Persistent and thorough Orderly and organized Neat and tidy Economical Sees the problems Finds creative solutions Needs to finish what he or she starts Likes charts, graphs, figures, lists	Competent and steady Peaceful and agreeable Has administrative ability Mediates problems Avoids conflicts Good under pressure Finds the easy way
F R I E N D S	Makes friends easily Loves people Thrives on compliments Seems exciting Envied by others Doesn't hold grudges Apologizes quickly Prevents dull moments Likes spontaneous activities	Has little need for friends Will work for group activity Will lead and organize Is usually right Excels in emergencies	Makes friends cautiously Content to stay in background Avoids causing attention Faithful and devoted Will listen to complaints Can solve others' problems Deep concern for other people Moved to tears with compassion Seeks ideal mate	Easy to get along with Pleasant and enjoyable Inoffensive Good listener Dry sense of humor Enjoys watching people Has many friends Has compassion and concern

WEAKNESSES

	Popular Sanguine	Powerful Choleric	Perfect Melancholy	Peaceful Phlegmatic

E M O T I O N S	Compulsive talker
	Exaggerates and
	    elaborates
	Dwells on trivia
	Can't remember names
	Scares others off
	Too happy for some
	Has restless energy
	Egotistical
	Blusters and complains
	Naive, gets taken in
	Has loud voice and laugh
	Controlled by
	    circumstances
	Gets angry easily
	Seems phony to some
	Never grows up
		Bossy
		Impatient
		Quick-tempered
		Can't relax
		Too impetuous
		Enjoys controversy
		    and arguments
		Won't give up when
		    losing
		Comes on too strong
		Inflexible
		Is not complimentary
		Dislikes tears and
		    emotions
		Is unsympathetic
			Remembers the
			    negatives
			Moody and depressed
			Enjoys being hurt
			Has false humility
			Off in another world
			Low self-image
			Has selective hearing
			Self-centered
			Too introspective
			Guilt feelings
			Persecution complex
			Tends to hypochondria
				Unenthusiastic
				Fearful and worried
				Indecisive
				Avoids responsibility
				Quiet will of iron
				Selfish
				Too shy and reticent
				Too compromising
				Self-righteous

W O R K	Would rather talk
	Forgets obligations
	Doesn't follow through
	Confidence fades fast
	Undisciplined
	Priorities out of order
	Decides by feelings
	Easily distracted
	Wastes time talking
		Little tolerance for
		    mistakes
		Doesn't analyze details
		Bored by trivia
		May make rash decisions
		May be rude or tactless
		Manipulates people
		Demanding of others
		End justifies the means
		Work may become his
		    or her god
		Demands loyalty in the
		    ranks
			Not people-oriented
			Depressed over
			    imperfections
			Chooses difficult work
			Hesitant to start projects
			Spends too much time
			    planning
			Prefers analysis to work
			Self-deprecating
			Hard to please
			Standards often too high
			Deep need for approval
				Not goal-oriented
				Lacks self-motivation
				Hard to get moving
				Resents being pushed
				Lazy and careless
				Discourages others
				Would rather watch

F R I E N D S	Hates to be alone
	Needs to be center
	    stage
	Wants to be popular
	Looks for credit
	Dominates
	    conversations
	Interrupts and doesn't
	    listen
	Answers for others
	Fickle and forgetful
	Makes excuses
	Repeats stories
		Tends to use people
		Dominates others
		Decides for others
		Knows everything
		Can do everything better
		Is too independent
		Possessive of friends
		    and mate
		Can't say, "I'm sorry"
		May be right, but
		    unpopular
			Lives through others
			Insecure socially
			Withdrawn and remote
			Critical of others
			Holds back affection
			Dislikes those in
			    opposition
			Suspicious of people
			Antagonistic and
			    vengeful
			Unforgiving
			Full of contradictions
			Skeptical of
			    compliments
				Dampens enthusiasm
				Stays uninvolved
				Is not exciting
				Indifferent to plans
				Judges others
				Sarcastic and teasing
				Resists change

Reprinted by permission from Florence Littauer, *After Every Wedding Comes a Marriage* (Eugene, Oreg.: Harvest House, 1981). All rights reserved.

You'll see we've added some descriptive adjectives to the personality types: Popular Sanguine, Perfect Melancholy, Powerful Choleric, and

Peaceful Phlegmatic. We find that these terms help people remember which characteristics are typically associated with those personality types. And while we call some of those characteristics *strengths*, it's important to note that, when carried to extremes, these traits *can* become weaknesses—or even compulsions, as shown in Table 2.

Table 2
Strengths Carried to Extremes

		Natural Strengths	Strengths carried to extremes	Compulsions
POPULAR	SANGUINE	Magnetic personality Entertaining storyteller Loves to go shopping Life of the party	Depends on charm and wit Constantly talking Buys and charges irrationally Too loud, too wild	Can become a con artist, bigamist Must be talking to feel secure Becomes a debt-laden shopaholic Makes fool of self, becomes party animal
PERFECT	MELANCHOLY	Schedule-oriented Knowledge on health and nutrition Neat, immaculate dresser Wants things done perfectly	Can't function without schedule Constant physical attention Can't go out until perfect Wants others to be perfect	Obsessed with punctuality May become hypochondriac Constant washing; has fetish about looks Nitpicks and criticizes constantly
POWERFUL	CHOLERIC	Born leader Decisive Quick and active Loves to work	Angry if people buck authority Decides for everyone Makes impulsive choices Works beyond the norm	Obsessed with power Manipulates own way Becomes irrational Becomes a workaholic
PEACEFUL	PHLEGMATIC	Low-key emotions Easygoing Cooperative Low motivation	Hides emotions Lets others decide Compromises standards Becomes lazy and laid-back	Blocks out all feeling Can't make any decisions Easily becomes a pawn Refuses to budge

Florence Littauer • CLASS Speakers • 1645 S. Rancho Santa Fe Road, Suite 102 • San Marcos, California 92069 • 619–471–0233

After you have transferred your checked words from the Personality Profile Test to the Personality Scoring Form, calculate your score and see which personality you score highest in. If you do not feel right about your results, consider these possibilities that may have distorted the profile:

1. You may have taken the test incorrectly. You should have made one check on each of forty lines (twenty strengths and twenty weaknesses). Sometimes people check no response or more than one response on each line, or they check only one response in each vertical column rather than on each horizontal line.

2. You transferred your responses incorrectly. For instance, instead of putting a 1 by the word *adaptable* on the scoring form you may have put the check in the same position on the scoring sheet as it was on the test, instead of on the same word.

3. You scored yourself as you would like to be, as others always wanted you to be, or as good Christian people should be instead of how you really are.

4. You are somewhat confused about who you really are, and you need help interpreting the score. Further assistance can be found in *Get a Life Without the Strife*.

NOTES

Chapter 1   Is This What Marriage Is Supposed to Be?
1. These "Communication Exercises for Husbands and Wives" comprise a chapter in our book *Get a Life Without the Strife* (Thomas Nelson, 1993).

Chapter 3   I Was Blind But Now I See
1. Fred Littauer, *The Promise of Healing* (Nashville: Thomas Nelson, 1994).

Chapter 5   Opposites Attract
1. This discussion of personalities is adapted from our book, *Get a Life Without the Strife* (Nashville: Thomas Nelson, 1993).

Chapter 9   "My Wife Has Little Desire to Be Intimate"
1. See Fred Littauer, *The Promise of Healing* (Nashville: Thomas Nelson, 1994), chapter 9.
2. Ibid.

Chapter 12   Does Your Wife Have an Abusive Husband?
1. These assessment questions are based on information developed by Donna Gardner and are used by permission.

Chapter 13   How Can the Husband Be the Head of the Wife?
1. Spiros Zodhiates, Th.D., *The Complete Word Study New Testament* (Chattanooga, Tenn.: AMG Publishers, 1991), 944.

Chapter 15   The Mark of a Man
1. Oswald Chambers, *My Utmost for His Highest* (New York: Dodd and Mead, 1935; reprinted 1965 by Barbour Books, Westwood, N.J.), September 21.
2. Ibid., November 30.
3. Ibid., April 2.

Chapter 16   The Life-Changing Power of Prayer

1. Fred Littauer, *The Promise of Healing* (Nashville: Thomas Nelson, 1994; originally published as *The Promise of Restoration* by Here's Life Publishing in 1990).

2. Note that some translations use the word *power* and others the word *authority*. Both are used here for emphasis and clarification.

3. The word *serpents* is used here "symbolically for satan. It eyes its objects attentively" (Spiros Zodhiates, *The Complete Word Study Dictionary: New Testament* (Chattanooga, Tenn.: AMG International, 1992).

4. "Scorpions are found in hot countries, where they lurk in decayed buildings and among the stones of old walls. Their sting is venomous, producing inflammation and swelling, but is seldom fatal unless treatment of the wound is neglected" (Zodhiates, *The Complete Word Study Dictionary: New Testament*). Scorpions are used here to symbolize evil spirits or demons.

Recommended Resource Order Form

Number Ordered   **Total**

____	1. *Wake Up, Women!* Florence Littauer	$11.00	____
____	2. *Wake Up, Men!* Fred Littauer	$11.00	____
____	3. *Get a Life Without the Strife,* Fred and Florence Littauer	$11.00	____
____	4. *Personality Plus,* Florence Littauer	$9.00	____
____	5. *Your Personality Tree,* Florence Littauer	$9.00	____
____	6. *Personalities in Power,* Florence Littauer	$9.00	____
____	7. *Personality Puzzle,* Florence Littauer and Marita Littauer	$10.00	____
____	8. *Freeing Your Mind from Memories That Bind,* Fred and Florence Littauer	$10.00	____
____	9. *The Promise of Healing,* Fred Littauer	$10.00	____
____	10. *Raising Christians Not Just Children,* Florence Littauer	$10.00	____
____	11. *Hope for Hurting Women,* Florence Littauer	$9.00	____
____	12. *How to Get Along with Difficult People,* Florence Littauer	$8.00	____
____	13. *Silver Boxes,* Florence Littauer (Hardback)	$13.00	____
____	14. *The Best of Florence Littauer,* compiled by M. Heavilin (Hardback)	$10.00	____
____	15. *Dare to Dream,* Florence Littauer	$10.00	____
____	16. *Make the Tough Times Count,* Florence Littauer	$10.00	____
____	17. *Your Personality Tree* Video Album, 8 half-hour lessons with book and study guide	$80.00	____
____	18. *Personality Profile Tests,* Fred Littauer (6 for $5.00)	$1.00	____
		SUBTOTAL	____

Shipping and Handling (please add $1.50 per book, $5.00 for the video album)   ____

California residents please add 7.75% sales tax   ____

TOTAL AMOUNT ENCLOSED (check or money order)   ____

CHARGE: MasterCard/Visa # _____

Name on card _____   Expiration Date _____

Make checks payable and mail to: CLASS Book Service
1645 S. Rancho Santa Fe Road #102
San Marcos, CA 92069

Payment plan may be made by sending three checks, each for one-third of total amount, one payable currently and the other two dated a month and two months later. International Orders: Please send checks in U.S. funds only and add $5.00 per book for shipping by air.